**WORLD BANK GROUP**
World Bank • IFC • MIGA

The World Bank Group and Public Procurement

AN INDEPENDENT EVALUATION

The World Bank Group and Public Procurement

AN INDEPENDENT EVALUATION

Contents

Abbreviations

CAS — Country Assistance Strategy

CDD — community-driven development

CPAR — Country Procurement Assessment Report

DPL — development policy loan

DPO — development policy operation

FCS — fragile and conflict-affected state

ICB — international competitive bidding

ICT — information and communications technology

IDF — institutional development fund

IEG — Independent Evaluation Group

IFI — international financial institution

INT — Integrity Vice Presidency

MAPS — Methodology for Assessing Procurement Systems

MDB — multilateral development bank

NCB — national competitive bidding

ORAF — Operational Risk Assessment Framework

PEFA — Public Expenditure and Financial Accountability

PPP — public-private partnership

P-RAMS — Procurement Risk Assessment Management System

UNCITRAL — United Nations Commission on International Trade Law

WBI — World Bank Institute

Acknowledgments

This report of the Independent Evaluation Group (IEG) was prepared by a core team led by Anjali Kumar, with major contributions provided by Nils Fostvedt, Prem Garg, Gita Gopal, Ian Hume, Eduardo Maldonado, Arvind Nair, Carla Pazce, Juliane Piecha, Robert Rothery, Swizen Rubbani, Justin Sigman, Kathryn Steingraber, Nadine Tushe, Christine Wallich, and Clay Wescott. Eleven country case studies were undertaken by Gian Casartelli, Jorge Claro, Ajay Guha, Rodolfo Hernandez, Jean-Jacques Lecat, Robert Rothery, Paul Schapper, and Christine Wallich. Additional contributions were provided by Jeanmarie Fath Meyer and S. Janakiram. Corky de Asis, Aimée Niane, Agnes Santos, and Lily Tsang provided administrative support.

The team gratefully acknowledges the support of managers and staff throughout the World Bank, especially in Operations Policy and Country Services departments and from both former and current regional procurement managers. IEG appreciates the many individual procurement staff throughout the Bank who have been generous with their time for surveys and interviews on aspects of the Bank's procurement system. Particular thanks are offered to the field-based procurement staff that provided assistance for field visits in Azerbaijan, Bangladesh, Ethiopia, Indonesia, Mexico, Morocco, the Philippines, Peru, Senegal, Tanzania, and Turkey, arranging meetings with key officials as well as private persons.

IEG also extends its thanks to other areas of the Bank consulted during the course of this evaluation: the Controllers, Economic Management, Institutional Integrity, Internal Audit, and Legal units. IEG also appreciates exchanges with the African Development Bank, the Asian Development Bank, the European Bank for Reconstruction and Development, the European Commission, the European Investment Bank, the Inter-American Development Bank, and the Organization for Economic Co-operation and Development, who shared their perspectives with the evaluation team, and its exchanges with academia at George Washington University, as well as Harvard University, the University of Florida, and Nottingham University, UK. The team also thanks client government counterparts, private sector suppliers, project implementation units, personnel from implementing agencies, and members of civil society who participated in IEG's surveys and interviews.

The evaluation benefited from constructive advice from external advisers and peer reviewers. Peer reviewers included Praful Patel (former Vice President, South Asia Region, and former Director, Infrastructure, Africa Region); Christiaan Poortman (former Vice President, Middle East and North Africa Region, World Bank, and current Senior Advisor at Transparency International and Chair of the Board of the Construction Sector Transparency Initiative); and Dr. Peter Trepte (Senior Fellow in Public Procurement Law, University of Nottingham). An external advisor provided overall guidance to the study—Professor Daniel Gordon, Associate Dean for Government Procurement Law at the George Washington University Law School.

The evaluation was conducted under the guidance of Nicholas York, Director, and Ali Khadr, Senior Manager, IEG Country, Corporate, and Global Evaluation, and Caroline Heider, IEG Director General.

Overview | HIGHLIGHTS

This evaluation of the World Bank's procurement systems and practices by the Independent Evaluation Group (IEG) informs the Bank's ongoing self-assessment of its procurement system and provides suggestions for future directions. Given the critical role of procurement in the efficiency of client countries' public expenditures, IEG first focuses (Volume I) on the extent to which the Bank has helped its clients develop better procurement capacity and improve their public procurement systems. Second, because World Bank operations are dominated by investment lending, Volume II of the report examines the extent to which Bank procurement guidelines and processes help support its own goals of competition, economy, efficiency, and transparency in the execution of Bank projects.

The Bank's wide array of efforts to support training and capacity building for procurement in client countries was fragmented and focused substantially on legal and regulatory reform. Reforms were supported by extensive use of policy-based lending and grants. There is limited evidence of systematic integration of procurement into the wider context of effective public expenditure. The Bank could better support capacity building for procurement through country-level strategies, the use of lending instruments adapted to providing hands-on assistance, and a fine tuning of its present diagnostic instruments.

Regarding development impact and the Bank's own lending, IEG finds that present Bank procurement guidelines (hereinafter referred to as Bank Guidelines) are broadly adequate instruments for Bank lending, including new areas of lending. IEG finds that there is need for review of select provisions, for example, on consultant selection or new and complex forms of procurement, such as in information and technology projects or public-private partnerships (PPPs). Bank procurement processes, in contrast, are time consuming and have posed difficulties because of inflexibilities in interpretation. Process change requires better monitoring, clear standards, and changes in incentives that would lead to the exercise of reasonable judgment and less risk aversion.

Looking at the potential for greater use of client countries' own procurement systems, some country clients point out gains from alleviating the need to maintain parallel systems. However, private suppliers want the World Bank to retain its role to ensure a level playing field, greater transparency in selection, and perceptions of higher levels of recourse. There is scope for the Bank to move further toward using country systems, on an incremental basis, in line with the approach adopted by global partners, taking into account its own risk assessments, country counterpart views, agency capabilities, and the views of the private sector. There is a need to consider how assurance could be provided that there would be no change to the Bank's legal remedies and no change in existing rights and obligations concerning fraud and corruption.

The Bank has a highly articulated set of instruments to manage fiduciary risk that have been strengthened in recent years. More integrated risk management systems and a greater focus on risk, as opposed to value, could reduce the need for oversight through prior review. Instruments could be fine tuned and the balance between the use of specific tools could be revisited, especially in the light of a risk-efficiency trade-off.

Finally, there is a significant need to improve Bank procurement processes in two areas: the setting of monitorable service standards and the introduction and use of procurement monitoring tools. These are imperative to help the Bank track the achievement of procurement goals such as economy, efficiency, and value for money. With such tools the Bank could make major global contributions to information on markets, suppliers, and prices, thus contributing to open data, benchmarking, and knowledge objectives.

Motivation and Principal Focus

Good public procurement practices are a major determinant of the effectiveness of public expenditure. Effective procurement policies enable better use of government budgets and are therefore an essential element of the Bank's poverty reduction focus. Equally, sound public procurement in countries is a prerequisite for the Bank's new lending instrument, the Program for Results, which makes use of national procurement policies. Moreover, Bank development policy loans (DPLs) are disbursed through national budgets. Thus, more effective public procurement may allow procurement practices in Bank lending to be unified across investment and policy-based lending and harmonized with other donors.

World Bank operations are dominated by investment lending. Bank procurement policies and processes affect the development impact of Bank lending and influence public procurement practices. The Bank seeks to ensure that its funds are used for the purpose intended and that they support development effectively and efficiently. Thus, the extent to which Bank investment lending procurement policies support the effectiveness of Bank lending have a deep influence on development outcomes.

Based on these factors, two overarching questions form the core of this evaluation:

• To what extent has the Bank helped its clients develop better procurement capacity and improve their public procurement systems? (addressed in Volume I of the present evaluation)

• To what extent does the application of Bank procurement guidelines in its investment lending help support its own development effectiveness objectives, in terms of fostering economy, efficiency, and transparency in the execution of Bank projects? (addressed in Volume II of this evaluation)

IEG's evaluation parallels an intensive Bank management review of its procurement function. It is motivated by the need to respond to a range of internal and external changes in the Bank's procurement environment, in terms of country capacity, supplier patterns, and emerging global practices in public procurement. IEG's evaluation is intended to inform management's review and contribute to the formulation of specific proposals for change.

Evaluation Scope and Questions

BUILDING PROCUREMENT CAPACITY

Strengthening national procurement systems refers here to the full set of institutional arrangements—the rules, norms, and procedures, both formal and informal—that govern public procurement, as well as the human resources organized to undertake public procurement transactions. Bank contributions to this process have taken the form of both advisory services and support through lending. IEG reviews the nature and quality of diagnostic work as well as loans focused on procurement reform and their impact in terms of results.

Procurement diagnostics were supported first through the Bank's Country Procurement Assessment Reports (CPARs) and later through the Methodology for Assessing Procurement Systems (MAPS) developed by the Development Assistance Committee of the Organisation for Economic Co-operation and Development. More integrated diagnostics of public procurement and public financial management systems have also been attempted, notably through the Public Expenditure and Financial Accountability (PEFA) instrument.

Support for strengthening national procurement systems has also been offered through some Bank lending operations, notably through development policy operations (DPOs) focused on public sector reform, which sometimes include procurement reform in their scope. The Bank also had some rare investment loans with a significant focus on procurement. And numerically significant, though small in value, were trust-funded institutional development fund (IDF) grants for procurement support. In addition, normal Bank investment lending in various sectors frequently provided procurement capacity-building support to project implementation units to encourage learning by doing. IEG's analysis of Bank support for capacity development reviews the relevance and quality of its support and the extent to which it has contributed to sustained results.

IEG also evaluates the extent to which the Bank contributed to the convening of global fora and the formulation of global norms on procurement. It was expected, under the aid reform agenda, that harmonization in procurement would lead to the development of standardized diagnostics for assessing countries' procurement systems. Working groups of the heads of procurement of international financial institutions (IFIs) also made efforts to prepare standardized bidding documents and to share policy positions in specialized aspects of procurement. Specific evaluation questions underpinning the first pillar of the evaluation are therefore:

- To what extent have Bank country departments supported the strengthening of client procurement systems, through diagnostic and advisory work and non-lending technical assistance?

- What is the quality of the advisory services offered, and what have the results been?

- Has the Bank been able to integrate advisory work in procurement within a framework of public financial management and efficient public expenditure?

- To what extent has the Bank been able to provide support for procurement system reform through its development policy and investment lending platforms?

- To what extent has the Bank been able to coordinate/harmonize its procurement processes with other development partners in accordance with the global aid effectiveness agenda, and how much has it been able to adopt useful elements from other multilateral development banks (MDBs)/IFIs in its own procurement systems?

CONTRIBUTING TO DEVELOPMENT EFFECTIVENESS IN BANK LENDING

Core principles in the Bank Guidelines for procurement refer to economy and efficiency, competition (equal opportunity for all bidders), and transparency, as well as encouragement to the development of domestic markets. In the evaluation, IEG therefore looks at the effectiveness of current Bank procurement systems in terms of the achievement of these underlying principles, including, among other things, reviewing the extent to which there may be trade-offs in their achievement.

In the light of this, IEG also reviews the Bank's pilot effort to move toward the use of country systems in procurement; the factors explaining the outcomes of the Bank's initial attempts; and considerations going forward, including approaches adopted by other IFIs and bilateral organizations and the views of client governments and private sector stakeholders.

IEG reviews the Bank's present contributions toward supporting the full upstream and downstream chain of the procurement process. And in terms of new directions, IEG explores present and possible future contributions to sustainable procurement and the extent to which there is scope for reflecting value-for-money principles in Bank procurement.

Bank lending has evolved in directions not envisaged by its present procurement framework. Community-driven development (CDD) projects pose particular questions, as they give control of procurement decisions to community groups. The Bank is also providing more support in complex areas such as information and communications technology (ICT), where its traditional separation of goods, works, and consultancy services is less distinct and where assumptions of buyers' prior knowledge of the best systems is open to question. PPPs—where the Bank contributes financing to projects that are not wholly under the client countries' government but also involve private financing—also raise questions in terms of the procurement methods that apply. And the Bank has been making efforts to step up support to fragile and conflict-affected states (FCS), which have particularly challenging environments for procurement. IEG reviews the extent to which current Bank procurement is equipped for Bank lending in these areas.

Risk management is a key element of procurement, to ensure that funds are used for their intended purposes. A mainstay of the management of procurement-related risk in Bank-financed projects has been an interlocking set of risk thresholds, for review of, and "no objection" to, a significant part of contracts. Other elements of the risk management framework include its recently formalized project-level procurement risk assessment—the P-RAMS (Procurement Risk-Assessment Management System) tool—and post-procurement reviews. The Bank's Integrity Vice Presidency (INT) department also maintains data that flag potential risk.

IEG evaluates the effectiveness of the spectrum of risk management tools currently deployed. There is a perception among staff that increased attention to potential corruption in procurement practices has resulted in more intensive project-level scrutiny, suggesting a trade-off between increased transparency and efficiency. IEG reviews the outcomes of the present system, in terms of identifying and correcting risk.

Finally, IEG evaluates the efficiency of the procurement process at the Bank, in terms of the information tools and systems available. IEG explores the reasons for oft-cited procurement delays through an analysis of elapsed time at various stages of the process and factors that may affect time taken. Last, IEG points to new ways of increasing efficiency through new procurement modalities and evaluates the present use of such tools in the Bank.

Evaluative questions for the second pillar are:

- How efficient/effective have the Bank's present investment lending procurement systems been, as perceived by Bank staff, country clients, and other stakeholders?

- To what extent has the Bank been able to move toward the use of country systems, as envisaged in the aid effectiveness agenda?

- To what extent is contract management incorporated in Bank procurement systems? To what extent are new approaches to procurement, such as sustainable procurement or value for money, taken into account in the Bank's procurement policies?

- To what extent has the Bank's present procurement system accommodated the evolving needs of Bank lending, for example, in areas such as CDD projects, PPPs, and ICT projects? To what extent has the Bank's present procurement system facilitated Bank engagement in FCSs?

- Are current risk-mitigation measures (thresholds for prior review, the postreview system, and so forth) effective?

- Have new risk management tools such as the P-RAMS qualitatively improved the Bank's overall risk management framework?

- What is the efficiency of the procurement process, in terms of the distribution and utilization of Bank procurement resources? How could efficiency be enhanced?

METHODOLOGY

IEG used both qualitative and quantitative methods in this evaluation. Structured questionnaires for portfolio analysis and interviews used category building and scoring to enable summarizing and comparison. Quantitative data sets were constructed and reviewed using spreadsheets. Where data permitted, IEG undertook simple statistical correlations and linear regression analyses to examine the association of procurement modalities with procurement outcomes.

In some areas, Bank procurement data were not available in a manner that could be extracted for analysis. Data across regions were often not comparable. Some core parameters on procurement functions are not tracked across all regions. As a result, IEG had to construct its own, sometimes partial, data sets. Findings are subject to this caveat.

One methodological challenge was the measurement of effectiveness of Bank interventions for country procurement capacity development. IEG synthesized and triangulated information from (i) time-ordered sequences of policy information from a variety of procurement system diagnostic and benchmarking studies; (ii) reports on lending operations, describing their goals and objectives as well as interim or final status and achievements; and (iii) information from country case studies, including structured and open-ended survey information.

Findings: Volume I
BUILDING PROCUREMENT CAPACITY AND SYSTEMS

Although the Bank has undertaken myriad procurement building efforts in almost all client countries, there has been an absence of strategic planning for procurement capacity building, and these efforts have been fragmented. There was early emphasis on diagnostic work, and the Bank's CPARs provided good foundations for reform. Diagnostics have been recently dominated by the MAPS instrument, which is not well adapted to offer forward-looking roadmaps or insights on the functioning of the procurement market. IEG finds that modest reform has been achieved in most cases, although there have been substantial or better results in two-fifths of the cases reviewed. Reviews of procurement, viewed through the public finance lens of the PEFA instrument, do not suggest a close integration of procurement within the public expenditure management framework.

There has been an orientation, in implementation of the recommendations of diagnostics, toward legal and institutional reform, perhaps appropriately for the early phases of procurement system development. As a consequence, the DPL became the Bank's principal lending instrument for procurement reform. The DPL is an instrument that may not be well adapted to support the second tier of procurement reforms that most Bank client countries now face. Bank support in the form of technical assistance for building procurement capacity has been scarce. IDF grants were the primary vehicle of technical support, but their small size and uncertain allocations have made them an unreliable instrument for building procurement capacity. Support for reform provided by the Bank's procurement anchor has been supplemented by programs offered by the World Bank Institute (WBI). Though this has been carefully handled to avoid overlap, it raises questions in terms of building integrated programs of country-level support.

COUNTRY STRATEGIES

IEG's analysis of Country Assistance Strategy (CAS) reports over the past decade reveals that Bank management had a high level of awareness of procurement-related issues and the need for support to building capacity. Issues relating to integrity and transparency were also frequently discussed, market development less so. However, there was a loose translation of priorities from procurement discussions in country strategies to specific actions, in the country work program for procurement reform. Most of the attention, especially initially, focused on existing or planned diagnostics. The Bank's CPARs were given a great deal of attention in CASs; other diagnostic instruments received negligible attention. The Bank paid limited attention to finding vehicles that would provide hands-on support for building findings into the work program.

The bulk of Bank budgetary resources were devoted to support for transactional procurement, for project implementation—far more than support for analytical or advisory work. Available data suggest that limited resources were allocated for procurement capacity building; furthermore, there was a decline over time in resources provided to support procurement-related analytic and advisory assistance after 2007, after diagnostic updates ceased to be mandated.

Quality and Coverage

The Bank made substantial efforts to build procurement systems in the early 2000s through its advisory work. These efforts consisted, in the first instance, of conducting CPARs to review the framework for procurement, especially in terms of legal and institutional aspects and to recommend reforms.

Once CPARs ceased to be mandated, and because MAPS was used for the Bank's country systems experiment, their frequency declined. To some extent, this was counterbalanced by the increased use of MAPS. Yet overall, the frequency of diagnostic exercises declined, so in some major borrower countries the Bank's procurement work is perceived to have lost some depth and traction over time, although in other countries, staff point out that the existing stock of knowledge was adequate.

There is much overlap in core areas, but CPAR guidelines addressed areas intended for Bank country dialogue, notably pointing out differences relative to the Bank, as required for project lending, and incorporating flexibility to address country-specific issues, and including action plans for improving procurement. MAPS assessments benefited from their rigid framework as a tool for benchmarking and comparison, and some enjoyed greater country ownership, as they were not Bank-mandated.

Although MAPS exercises had more consistent structure, they were deemed to provide a "snapshot" of the system, rather than a roadmap for reform. Their limitations in terms of describing the functioning of a procurement system partly reflect the limited use of the MAPS performance indicators—possibly reflecting their complexity in environments of limited data availability. The recent integration of MAPS into CPARs in some countries (Ethiopia, for example) is perhaps the most useful diagnostic tool, acknowledging the positive features of each. The PEFA instrument used by the Bank is also useful, although in limited areas and for high-level assessments of procurement and other aspects of public financial management related to procurement.

More than half of Bank reports were found to be substantially well structured. CPARs were more prone to scattered discussion, sometimes of critical topics; MAPS reports lagged in terms of preparing clear and actionable strategies. All reports focused more on the existence of structures and regulations but were supported by little data on how systems worked in practice. The area of accessibility (whether or not the laws were published and available to interested parties) was often neglected.

IEG found that risk assessments were limited in both MAPS and CPARs. Where there was a risk assessment, it rarely distinguished between the risk for Bank projects and that for public procurement generally. This may have reflected the fact that other Bank tools undertook at least project-level risk assessments for procurement risk.

Earlier CPARs had less coverage of the integration of procurement into the budgeting, planning, and audit process and the existence and dissemination of monitoring and procurement statistics, although these areas were both consistently covered by the MAPS framework. Coverage improved in later CPARs.

IEG also found that the Bank usually undertook assessments of overall borrower capacity levels related to procurement. The assessments pointed toward constraints from the lack of established career paths in procurement, which was worsened by high turnover. Reports fell short of specifics, such as the financial sustainability of training.

Although legislation related to corruption tended to be addressed in reports, there was little discussion of the existence or application of enforcement mechanisms. Coverage of the complaints process and the appeals mechanism varied greatly in subjects covered, although the lack of an appeal process or proper complaint mechanism was a recurrent theme.

Issues related to the performance of the public procurement market were relatively neglected by earlier CPARs; in later reports, however, they were for the most part given due importance by the MAPS framework. The Bank often discussed, and strongly endorsed, the use of electronic systems to collect and disseminate statistics, although the Bank itself has faced major challenges in this area.

Finally, an examination of PEFAs shows that there was little attention to public sector management issues such as cash planning or commitment reporting.

Follow-Up and Results

Overall results, measured in terms of the extent to which action plans in Bank diagnostics were implemented, were mixed: high or substantial implementation was found in around two-fifths of the countries surveyed, especially in the legal and institutional framework (Figure 1). These findings are robust to additional analyses undertaken specifically through the lens of public expenditure management. And more comprehensive and focused diagnostics such as MAPs and CPARs have been more important in terms of getting results. There is no evidence of improvements in procurement performance being specifically linked to public expenditure management instruments such as PEFAs or public expenditure reviews.

FIGURE 1 Moderate Results in Most Areas

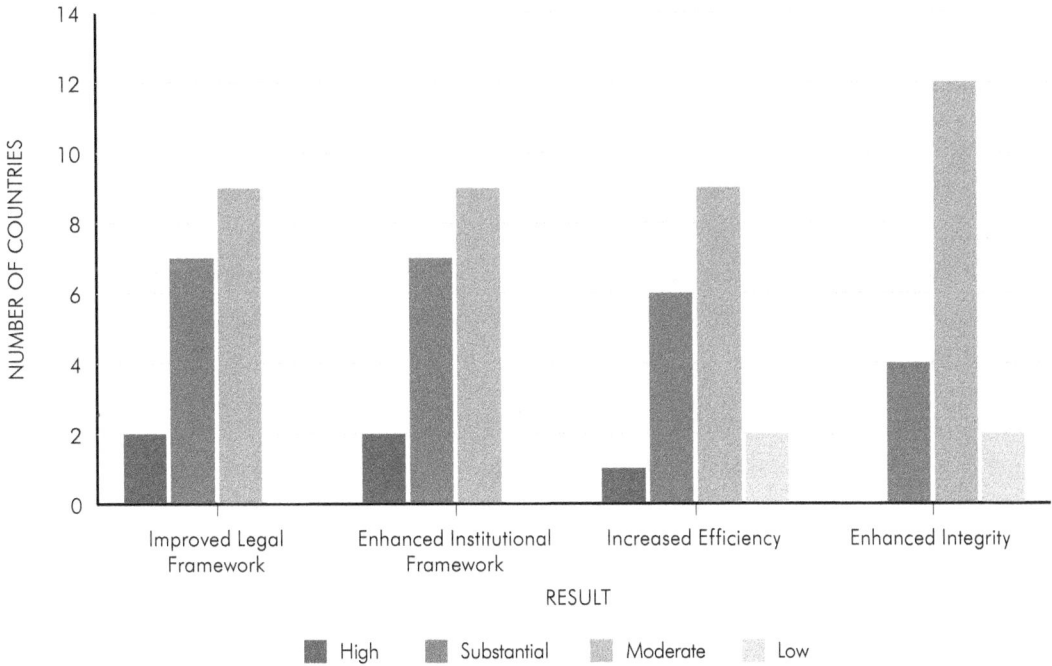

SOURCE: IEG analysis.

Success was focused on "first-generation" results, in terms of passage of laws and establishment of institutions, especially in the earlier part of the period. The Bank tended to focus on the implementation of rules and requirements that add processes, but not necessarily commensurate value or transparency. Findings based specifically on the PEFA instrument also show that results in formal, rather than functional, areas predominated. Field visits corroborate this finding.

In many countries where the Bank's work was more influential, there may have been greater country capacity (Mauritius, Morocco, the Philippines, and Turkey). Yet government commitment is also critical, as illustrated by progress achieved in countries such as Rwanda.

Political economy matters. The legislature may be willing to pass a law for procurement, but it may not represent wide stakeholder consensus. This is a consideration when the achievement of results is staked on policy-based lending instruments.

A caveat to the preceding findings is the lack of quantitative information or statistical data on procurement "compliance and performance" type indicators (as described by MAPS); this lack necessarily limited the analysis. Another limitation, in decentralized countries such as Mexico, is that assessments are typically limited to national levels, whereas states may have their own procurement systems.

In field visits IEG also found that in most countries, at least some actions were taken, based on the recommendations of Bank diagnostic work. Yet in 10 of 11 countries, there was an absence of a comprehensive country-level procurement capacity-building strategy and action plan. Only a few programs for human capacity development looked at longer-term sustainability issues.

Field visits were a valuable source of information on the outcomes of Bank programs for human capacity development in procurement. They illustrate that limited success achieved in procurement capacity building is due to endemic country issues as much as to Bank-related issues. Although the Bank attempted some procurement capacity building in most countries, it was mostly with a focus on immediate needs for implementing Bank lending. There has also been on-the-job training and mentoring of local government staff. Bank personnel are stretched, with emphasis in their work on transactional commitments.

There is some perception that the Bank is not equipped to offer "cutting edge" advice, for example, in new modalities or in areas of complex procurement; however, it may be an issue of Bank staff time allocation and lack of training rather than Bank staff capacity or helpfulness, which was generally widely appreciated. Turnover of Bank staff and consultants and time-consuming and protracted Bank hiring processes were also mentioned as limiting the development of long-term procurement capacity.

On the government side, resources are invariably stretched, civil service salaries are low, and staff turnover is typical. The lack of recognition of procurement as a professional stream is an impediment that some governments have tried to address. However, building procurement capacity is also an integral part of a wider civil service capacity-building exercise, and it cannot be developed in isolation of the overall civil service cadre.

SUPPORT TO PROCUREMENT CAPACITY THROUGH LENDING

Implementation of the Bank's diagnostic recommendations was often supported by policy-based lending (DPLs including poverty reduction support credits), which was seen as a successful instrument for taking the procurement reform agenda forward. The Bank supported procurement reform throughout the evaluation period with procurement-related conditions of

FIGURE 2 Operations Supporting Procurement Capacity: DPLs, ILs, and IDF Grants (numbers)

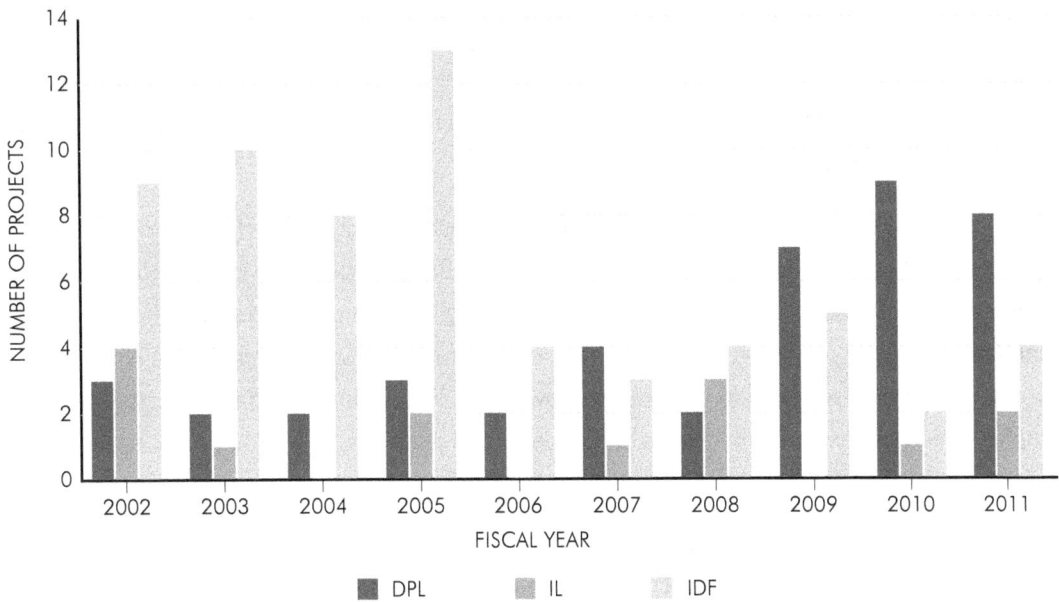

SOURCE: IEG analysis.
NOTE: DPL = development policy loan; IL = investment loan; IDF = institutional development fund grant.

triggers embedded in a substantial number of multisector or public sector management DPLs, often combined with numerous small IDF grants, but with scarcely any technical assistance-focused investment lending (Figure 2).

In only one country visited—Bangladesh—did the Bank use investment lending to support building procurement systems and institutional capacity. To some degree this also reflects the reluctance on the part of some countries to borrow for technical assistance, preferring the use of grants instead.

Bank loans addressed a substantial range of issues, albeit with concentration, especially in DPOs, on the legal framework as well as institutional strengthening. DPOs paid less attention to efficiency issues or to more advanced procurement market strengthening or longer-term capacity development. And there was little focus, except in perfunctory terms, on the integration of public procurement into the wider framework of public financial management.

There was heavy focus on legislative and institutional development issues, but there is some evidence of progress toward "second-generation" issues of improving markets and procurement efficiency, although this has remained limited.

Hands-on capacity building and market development issues were tackled by IDF grants, often with some success, but their smaller size and uncertain nature made them less reliable vehicles for the operationalization of procurement reform.

Field visits suggest that by and large, the main source of ongoing support for building procurement systems and capacity in country through Bank lending was indirect rather than direct—by means of within-project support to implementing agencies to help them undertake project-specific procurement in the context of individual investment projects. This was supplemented with hands-on support provided by World Bank procurement staff to implementing agencies for the execution of specific transactions.

At the most basic level, the within-project training and hands-on implementation support provided by Bank procurement staff did not have adequate resources—in only one country visited could a separate earmarked work program agreement allocation be identified for procurement capacity building, as separate from transactional procurement work of the procurement unit.

Many countries had mutually interlocking patterns of support for procurement reform through a combination of DPOs, IDF grants, and investment lending. This appears to have been beneficial.

There was limited scope for changes from a single lending operation—engagement over time has been essential and the pace of reform is slow. There is a value in undertaking reform through programmatic, longer-term, or repeat instruments.

INTEGRATING SUPPORT ACROSS THE WORLD BANK GROUP

There are anecdotal examples of good collaboration though the lens of public sector management, though there are also instances where collaboration has been limited. IEG finds that good collaboration usually reflects circumstances with one or more similar elements: ample funding, support from governments and senior regional management, and staff from different practices that work well together. It is desirable to institutionalize collaboration through better incentives and rewards for knowledge sharing and cooperation. Preparation and dissemination of information by the Bank on how good procurement actually helps expenditure management would help motivate staff as well as clients.

The WBI is on track to make valuable contributions to developing procurement capacity. There has been limited overlap between WBI and the Bank's procurement anchor. Many services were demand driven, and WBI exercised selectivity in choosing its entry points and instruments. However, because of limited trust-funded resources, it is not clear how work can be scaled up. A key area of WBI work is support to nongovernmental organizations and civil society organizations in procurement oversight. If countries develop this capacity, they will have an important skill for good oversight of public procurement.

Despite careful management to avoid obvious overlap, it remains a question of whether the present distribution of work across the Poverty Reduction and Economic Management Vice Presidency, WBI, and the Operations Policy and Country Services anchor facilitates the achievement of maximum effectiveness from the perspective of developing country procurement capacity. For example, country clients expect Bank procurement staff to provide leadership in areas such as e-procurement, notwithstanding relevant and useful training courses in this area. An integrated overall country approach is desirable.

CONTRIBUTING TO GLOBAL GOOD PRACTICE IN PROCUREMENT

Over more than a decade, the Bank has played a lead role in advancing the global agenda of building and harmonizing good practice in public procurement, with many successes. The Bank's work is widely recognized and appreciated by development partners and client countries.

The Bank has been instrumental in developing assessment tools, starting with its own CPAR and helping develop the MAPS tool. Less successful have been efforts to mainstream procurement reform within the context of financial management reform and overall public expenditure management. Additionally, the Bank has been viewed by some global partners as unwilling to engage the private sector.

The Bank's efforts to coordinate with partners on reform, capacity building, and alignment of practices are varied: they are substantial in Mexico and the Philippines (where the Bank leads a multidonor coordination effort) but negligible in Indonesia and Turkey (in the former, the Bank has relinquished the lead role to the Australian Agency for International Development and the Millennium Challenge Corporation).

Practices of the Bank and other IFIs are largely aligned, with differences mainly related to their different memberships (hence the Bank's insistence on worldwide procurement, in contrast to some regional development banks and bilaterals) and different sanctioning procedures. Although differences are few, they can be problematic on cofinanced projects, where the Bank requires the use of its procedures.

Findings: Volume II

On the whole, country clients, the private sector, and Bank staff agree that the Bank's present procurement guidelines for goods and works are reasonably successful in securing fairness, competition, and transparency in Bank procurement. Nevertheless, there may be scope for improvement in certain details. One particular area is the "consulting guidelines," where it was found during country visits that inappropriate selection methods led to poor short lists, reduced participation by qualified consultants, and long selection processes.

There is less comfort with Bank procurement processes, especially with regard to time taken, flexibility, and consistency; this discomfort can lead to losses in development effectiveness. Focus on compliance in transactions may distract from a focus on outcomes and may not ensure the containment of fraud and corruption, which is to some extent a systemic rather than project-level issue.

THE USE OF COUNTRY SYSTEMS FOR PROCUREMENT

Given the pros and cons of current Bank procurement rules and processes, IEG reviewed recent Bank efforts to move toward greater use of country systems and the extent to which this could be taken forward in the future. As a prelude, it should be noted that many Bank client country procurement systems today bear a strong resemblance to Bank systems, reflecting past decades of Bank support for the development of country procurement systems. Many processes also reflect global practice, such as the United Nations Commission on International Trade Law (UNCITRAL) rules. Thus, although most countries have specific areas of difference relative to the Bank, radical differences in structure are rare.

There are many interpretations of the extent and degree to which country systems may be used. Consequently, different approaches are adopted by IFIs and bilateral donors. The Bank developed its own approach toward piloting the use of country systems—an effort characterized by rigor but also minutiae. Most candidate countries showed varying degrees of difference from Bank Guidelines (Figure 3).

Such a focus may have led to the termination of the Bank's efforts to pilot the use of country systems; however, lessons have been learned about areas of difference between current Bank policy and policy prevailing in various country systems. Most country systems have some differences from the Bank, but some differences have greater materiality than others, in terms of underlying Bank principles, touching on core principles of promoting competition and market access; other differences impact less on such principles, and there may be scope for flexibility.

FIGURE 3 Procurement Systems of UCS Participants Relative to the Bank—IEG Scores

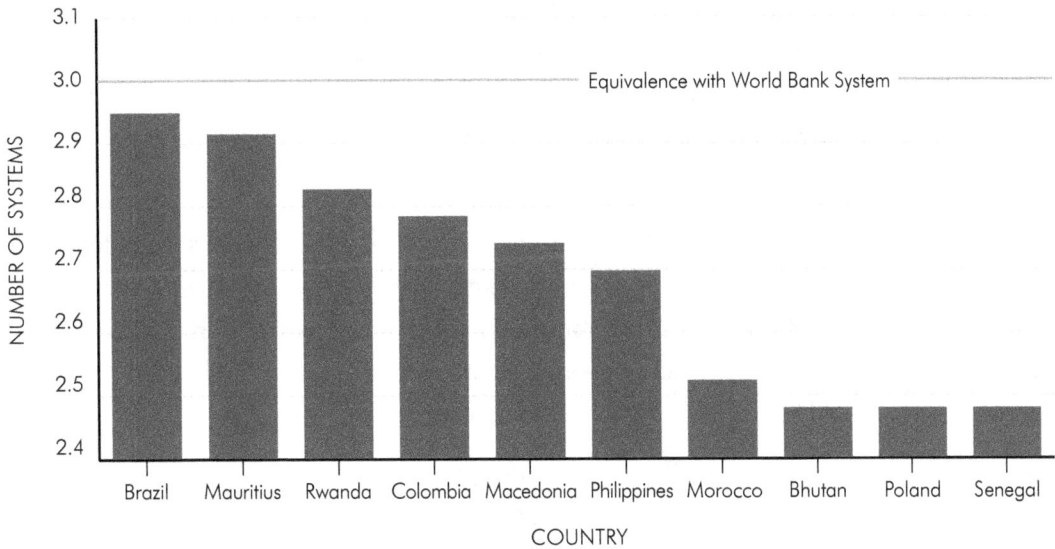

SOURCE: IEG analysis of UCS documents.
NOTE: Based on IEG scoring methodology. UCS = use of country systems.

Bank procurement systems (as embodied in its Guidelines) are generally well tolerated by both client governments and private sector suppliers; however, problems with the implementation of such systems, that is, with Bank procurement processes, are abundant.

Country clients have mixed views on the adoption of countries' own procurement systems, and this may reflect ambiguity in the concept of use of country systems that would benefit from clarification. This is especially true with regard to the extent to which they would also include, for example, Bank engagement in the procurement process, in fiduciary oversight, or in legal recourse (complaint review, dispute resolution, and so forth).

On one hand, clients in the government and implementing agencies see benefits in the adoption of country systems, which would reduce the need for countries to maintain parallel rules and train staff in two sets of guidelines. They point out gains from alleviating the need to maintain parallel systems, increasing opportunities for harmonizing across donors and building long term capacity applicable to all public sector purchasing, not only on account of Bank projects.

On the other hand, private sector suppliers prefer to use Bank systems. These are seen as assuring financing, mitigating corruption, and providing redress mechanisms. However, it is not clear to what extent this refers to differences in underlying procurement guidelines or to closer Bank engagement with contract award, payment, and fiduciary oversight. And among both sets of stakeholders, there is a preference for Bank rules, especially for the large value contracts for which Bank systems were designed.

One conclusion that may be drawn from these different voices is that the area of contention is not necessarily Bank systems versus country systems, but rather, the presence of the Bank, with its benefits of experience and transparency. The adjustment of Bank processes, to provide greater upstream and downstream support, raise efficiencies, and better define accountabilities, could help ease a move toward country systems.

The Inter-American Development Bank and proposed African Development Bank use of country system programs contrast with the Bank's pilot, avoiding the "all-or-nothing" approach and striving to gradually move to full use of country systems through a measured process involving partial use, conditional acceptance, agreed improvements, and considerations of intent and objectives. Their programs illustrate that it is not necessary to assess or approve the entire country system—subsystems or components may be approved. Approval might be limited to administrative entities such as national government agencies, specific sectors such as infrastructure or health, or a particular state agency. It could also be limited to particular types of procurement, such as goods and works, or consulting services, or to particular procurement methods or categories.

Moreover, it is possible to approve a system, or component of a system, if the intent of the requirement is met through other means—for example, if there is coverage outside the procurement law but under other acceptable legislation, such as for arbitration or dispute resolution. Where a mandatory requirement is not met, it can be accepted conditionally. And where nonapproval runs counter to the objective of contributing to project outcomes, a system may be approved with an attached requirement to address a deficiency.

Finally, in a move toward country systems, there would be a need to focus on governance outcomes related to integrity, oversight, and political interference. This would provide assurances that the Bank's legal remedies are available and that the broad spectrum of existing rights and obligations concerning fraud and corruption is maintained.

Upstream and Downstream Engagement in Procurement

There is scope for more Bank support upstream in the acquisitions phase of the procurement process, in terms of bringing specific skills to the process and closer integration with sectors.

There is also scope to review the role of the Bank in overall procurement planning and the integration of procurement in public budget management.

There is a clearly perceived need also for greater involvement downstream in contract management. Important information such as that on contract amendments, quantities received, and satisfactory delivery and performance, and so forth, is not available without such integration; this reduces the ability to monitor results on the ground and raises the possibility of fraud and corruption.

One question here is the role of different sets of players in the contract administration phase. It is not clear, first, whether or to what extent the support should be provided by Bank procurement staff, Bank task team leaders, technical experts, or national institutions that can provide support, whether hands on (project implementation agencies) or through oversight functions (such as a national audit office). In Bangladesh, for example, procurement staff felt that more engagement with contract management represents an oversight and advisory function for national execution, rather than a transfer of responsibility to the Bank. Among Bank staff, there is a need to review and resolve limitations in the present incentive structure, experience, and turnover of task team leaders. The role and extent of the Bank's procurement function will need to be considered relative to the roles of other agents in the country.

Equally, rights and obligations between the Bank and the country client need to be carefully balanced within the legal framework of Bank-client commitments. Contracts are made between a borrower/implementation agency and contractor, and the Bank is not a party to this. Most other countries and most international documents (such as the World Trade Organization Agreement on Government Procurement, the UNCITRAL model procurement law, and the European Union Procurement Directives) do not address contract performance or consider it a part of procurement.

Finally, the Bank could also fortify its support to countries (currently offered on a limited scale through the WBI) to develop civil society oversight of public procurement and contract execution.

DOMESTIC PREFERENCES

Most countries have elements of domestic preference in their procurement policies. Although the Bank Guidelines endorse the principle of developing domestic manufacturing and contracting capabilities, the prescribed domestic preference scheme is restrictive in scope, which may explain its limited use. To the extent that the Bank retains the objective to develop domestic capacity through its procurement system, it may wish to consider a broader approach to developing domestic supply capability.

There are areas where the current Bank policy may have unintended consequences that affect national consultants, for example, regional constraints on consultant short lists that limit capable domestic bidders even in the absence of limited external interest, thus potentially limiting overall competition. In fact, these provisions limit any consultant short lists to two from any one country. Although there are some provisions for flexibilities in this regard, including provisions for the participation of "national experts," they appear to be little used by task team leaders or clients.

Another consequence is the tendency for domestic consultants to enter into joint ventures with foreign partners to meet geographical diversification requirements. Available provisions in the Bank Guidelines for local expert staff are rarely used. A review of such areas would be desirable.

SUSTAINABLE PROCUREMENT

Regarding sustainable and environmentally aware procurement, Bank Guidelines and practices already offer many avenues to incorporate "green" considerations into the procurement process, although they are not systematically used. Guidance for sector and procurement staff would help expand this. There is scope for further clarification, especially in circumstances where the most sustainable outcome does not lead to the lowest cost. More guidance on the evaluation of nonquantifiable and nonmonetizable factors would also help.

In line with the Bank's environment policies and objectives, procurement policies could also explicitly state the need to incorporate environmental and energy efficiency factors into technical specifications and bid evaluation criteria.

The Bank needs to address the conditions around which it will accept country standards (ecolabeling) and environment-related laws and policies in Bank-funded procurement, so that it can maintain alignment with donors and with international practice.

VALUE FOR MONEY IN BANK PROCUREMENT

The principle of value for money is increasingly being explicitly incorporated into public procurement in many jurisdictions, with varying degrees of operational instruction and varying emphasis. Many aspects are already implicit in Bank procurement, and some are frequently used. Stronger direction could be given to staff and borrowers to fortify the adoption of such practices.

A number of the efficiency-increasing (and transaction cost-reducing) measures proposed here would expand value for money, in its broadest sense, as would better management of risk and the embracing of new procurement practices in frontier areas of Bank business. The Bank could explore greater use of new procurement modalities such as framework agreements (which limit the need for repeated new procurements of similar items); e-procurement; and in select circumstances, greater use of negotiation (which in complex areas such as information technology allows better specification of what is to be bought, through discussions between buyers and sellers). However, areas remain where—for reasons of open access or transparency—the Bank may prefer to maintain its present systems and practices.

CDDs and Procurement

Bank procurement systems appear to be capable of handling the needs of some areas, or modalities, of relatively new emphasis in Bank lending. CDD projects were one of the areas reviewed. Almost a quarter of Bank projects have some such elements, according to present nomenclature, and these appear to have a higher incidence of procurement issues than other projects.

However, looking more specifically at the subset of projects that actually deploy CDD methods—that is, community management of resources—procurement does not appear to be unusually problematic. Reported procurement problems have frequently related to the non-CDD components of those projects, for example, difficulties in procuring the consulting services and technical assistance needed to support implementation of the CDD components. Although the Bank's procurement guidelines appear to have appropriate flexibility for such projects, front-line staff have been hesitant to use them.

CDD projects would nevertheless benefit from implementation support to assist with lower procurement capacity at the community level. Post-Procurement Reviews could play a more important role in monitoring CDD projects. Finally, shifting the CDD paradigm so that communities are expected to deliver agreed outputs and outcomes rather than controls on procurement of inputs may also be a route to explore.

Procurement in Fragile and Conflict Situations

Increasing Bank engagement with countries in fragile and conflict situations, often as the fulcrum of multidonor trust funds, heightens Bank responsibility for effective procurement in these environments. Although issues related to procurement are pointed out in a number of country strategy reports in FCS countries, their frequency is not greater than similar issues raised for all countries.

The Bank offers flexibilities in procurement in such environments, many of which have been helpful and widely used. There was consensus on the frequent use and benefits of higher approval authority for procurement staff in the field, often up to the regional procurement manager level. There was also agreement on greater use of higher thresholds for national competitive bidding (NCB) and prior review; greater use of rapid procurement methods such as direct contracting (reportedly used most frequently), simple shopping, or use of prequalified consultants; and greater use of extension of contracts. Respondents indicated that three countries—the Democratic Republic of Congo, South Sudan, and Sudan—regularly used accelerated bidding and streamlined procedures and found them highly effective. Yet flexibilities have not always been used. Conversely, such flexibilities have also been used in operations that are not under special procedures.

Many flexibilities afforded for FCS procurement, such as greater delegation to field staff, greater choice over procurement methods, or higher thresholds, are consistent with overall findings of the present report and its proposals. Accordingly, the need for further special regimes for such operations or clients may diminish over time.

Finally, lack of country capacity and overall political economy considerations remain overarching concerns and may require reinforcing and supplementing through staff resources.

ICT Procurement

Bank systems for ICT procurement have improved recently, and the Bank Guidelines have permitted new flexibilities and clarifications that are well suited to the ICT process. Bank standard bidding documents for ICT projects, with their scoring process, Bank acceptance of two-stage bidding, and Bank approvals—when needed—of sole source and its clarification of conflicts of interest for consultants, are welcome moves.

Yet legacy difficulties remain, reflecting the adaptation of the present system from one designed for a very different purpose. The Bank's standard bidding documents are not user friendly and are not aligned with industry norms. Although the system has flexibilities, many are discretionary and there is hesitation to use them. The complex chain of clearance for "no objection" is compounded by approaches that use new or unusual processes and can lead to significant delay.

Task team leaders and procurement staff have a limited awareness of available flexibilities and hesitate to use them, in part because of risk aversion, but also because of a limited understanding of their benefits. Though the Bank has consistently offered advice and support for contract implementation, its interventions have been somewhat skewed toward upstream transactions. Nevertheless, better project design remains an issue, and this requires training and awareness building among team leaders. Finally, country capacity is sometimes—though not always—a constraint.

PPP Procurement

To the extent that the Bank's public sector–oriented procurement processes do not match the demands of PPP projects, this impedes uptake of PPP investments. In view of the need to leverage Bank resources in a world where private investment is a growing share of the total, better procurement systems for such situations are critical for the Bank. IEG finds that although there have been recent improvements, there are still significant remaining hurdles. In principle, the Bank accepts private investors' selection processes and standards for concessionaires, subject to the Bank's review, but there is ambiguity regarding the scope of the Bank's review and of standards it will accept. There is also ambiguity in situations where the Bank enters late and is not involved in the design (including the design of procurement processes) from the beginning.

Sometimes, procurement arrangements have been established by other investors, sometimes with larger financial stakes, where the Bank might be a minority investor. In such situations, its prerogative of requiring review and compliance is less evident. This also applies to on-lending arrangements, financing via investment funds, or other situations with numerous small investments under an umbrella arrangement. In these circumstances the Bank does not adequately recognize commercial confidentiality concerns that may make large players unwilling to share some information with a minor player, especially if they are considered commercially sensitive.

Even competitively selected concessionaires can enter into conflicted downstream agreements—and conversely those not competitively selected under their own rules, and so required to follow the Bank's procurement rules downstream, may pursue best value procurement. At present, the Bank does not have obvious methods of controlling downstream conflict of interest. It also lacks the means to provide guidance on contract management. PPPs are output-based, long-duration contracts where contract management may be as important as the process by which the contract is developed.

Country case studies illustrate frustration with the Bank's slow response. The Bank is seen as ill equipped to adapt to the procedures of others, especially where quick response is needed, for example, to round out a financing consortium.

Bank policy—although very similar to those of other MDBs—allows some negotiation, provided it is disclosed in the bidding documents. This practice differs from the European Union's competitive negotiation practices. To the extent that the degree to which negotiation is permitted to arrive at a PPP concession agreement differs across jurisdictions, the Bank may need to find a mechanism to accept local negotiation practices in certain circumstances.

MANAGING RISK

Viewing all aspects of the present review of procurement risk management, the overall conclusion is a qualified positive. In terms of *design*, the Bank has a highly articulated set of procurement risk management instruments that has been strengthened in recent years. However, its tools could be sharpened in focus, better integrated, and made better use of, not only in terms of data input but also in analysis of findings. And the balance between the use of specific tools could be revisited, especially in the light of a risk-efficiency trade-off.

In terms of *results*, most current measures of risk failure appear to be within acceptable levels of risk tolerance, based on (i) numbers of misprocurements declared each year, (ii) procurement complaints relative to bid awards, and (iii) INT referrals in relation to perceived fraud and corruption indicators in the procurement process. Ratios fall in ranges below 1–2 percent of contracts by number and value.

In terms of feedback and institutional *learning* from risk management tools and instances of risk failure, these are already objectives, as evidenced by the annual report on financial management and procurement. However, use of this material could be improved: at present the data are descriptive and compliance focused, and the notion of "risk failure" is only implicit.

There is limited analysis of the effectiveness or outcomes of pivotal risk management tools such as the procurement threshold system, the content of Post-Procurement Reviews, or data collected through the P-RAMS instrument, in terms of analyzing content, tracing trends, or correlating risk management and procurement outcomes.

In terms of its present risk management framework, the Bank puts considerable emphasis on ex ante risk controls through mechanisms such as prior review and clearance thresholds, which require prior review of contracts above certain values by procurement staff at increasing levels of seniority, depending on contract value. Yet findings show that prior review instruments at best partially reflect country or project risk and could thus be relied on less as risk control mechanisms (Figure 4).

FIGURE 4 Correlation of Prior Review Thresholds with CPIA Scores (2008 ICB Goods)

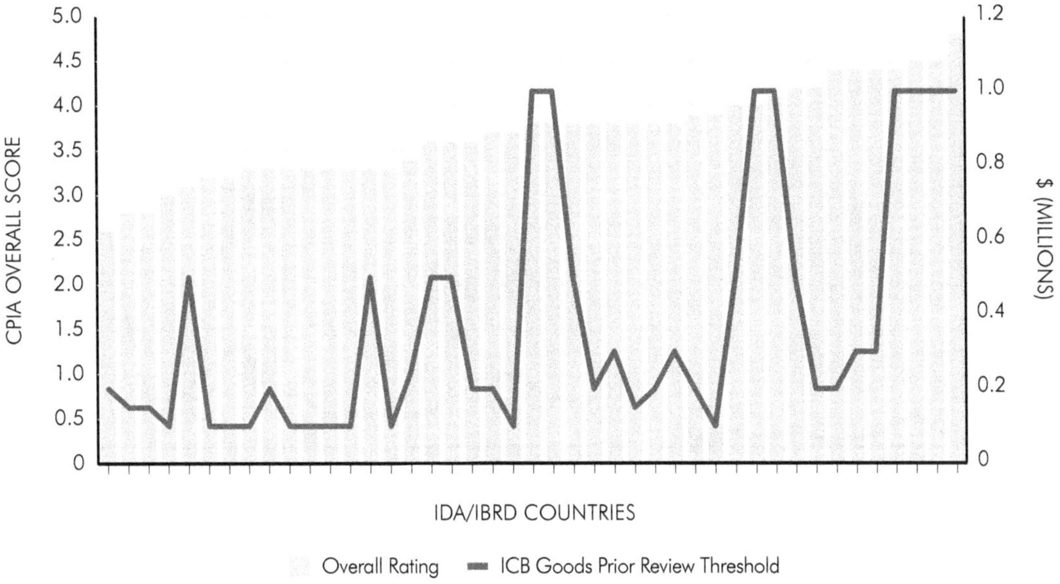

SOURCE: IEG analysis.
NOTE: CPIA = Country Policy and Institutional Assessment Indicator; IBRD = International Bank for Reconstruction and Development; ICB = international competitive bidding; IDA = International Development Association.

To the extent that the Bank chooses to use prior review thresholds, a shift in focus from value-based to risk-based thresholds is desirable. And to the extent that the Bank maintains "methods" thresholds, they could incorporate better use of market information. These measures could lead to greater cost-effectiveness in risk management and increased consistency of treatment of client countries.

The Bank effectively applies its most intensive and therefore slowest risk management process—prior review—to its most competitive and therefore potentially less risky procurement method contracts (especially, international competitive bidding—ICB—contracts, but also to some NCB contracts). There is likely to be scope to reduce the risk efficiency trade-off by reducing the share of prior-reviewed contracts and focusing prior review on the highest risk contracts. Additional risk that this may imply could be mitigated by better use of Post Procurement Reviews and Independent Procurement Reviews (IPRs). This need not imply an increase in their numbers, but rather a more strategic use of their findings.

FIGURE 5 Increase in the Number of P-RAMS Completed

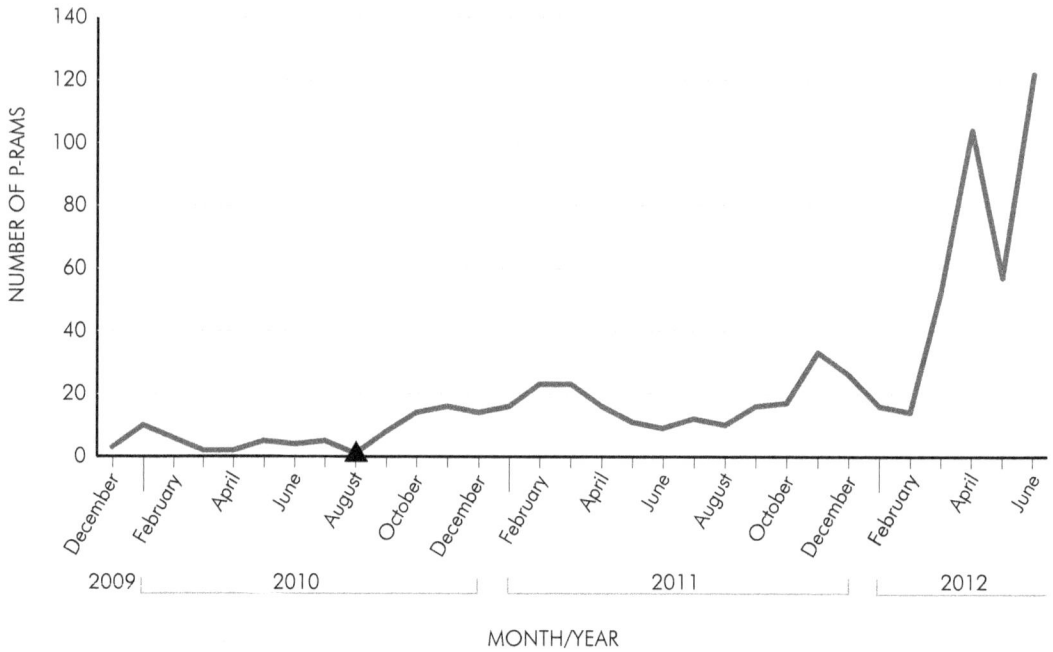

SOURCE: IEG calculations from P-RAMS database.
NOTE: P-RAMS = Procurement Risk Assessment Management System.

Bank procurement staff acknowledge that current review procedures are helpful for controlling fiduciary risk. Nevertheless, on balance, there was a view that current prior-review thresholds could be raised with beneficial impacts on workload and clearance time, and only limited impact on risk or competition. There is also a likely benefit from reviewing the way methods thresholds are set. Insistence on ICB, when good domestic capacity exists, has a cost in terms of longer process time and can oblige local firms to take up sometimes little warranted joint ventures, in those circumstances where conventional regional considerations apply to consultant short lists. This has to be weighed carefully against the benefits to additional competition that ICB brings.

The Bank recently introduced a new risk management tool, the P-RAMS. The extent to which P-RAMS has been deployed Bank-wide has significantly increased in recent months (Figure 5). P-RAMS is a well-intended effort to offer more focused and standardized assessment and mitigation of procurement risks. In principle, a key positive feature is its dynamic aspect, now beginning to be articulated. Yet undertaking P-RAMS with excessive frequency may be counterproductive. Although the linkage of P-RAMS to the Bank's new Operational Risk Assessment framework (ORAF) is indeed operating and should provide for some enhancement in the treatment of procurement risk in overall project risk, this potential impact has also been attenuated by ORAF's partial adoption.

On the less positive side, the P-RAMS template and process can be cumbersome and time consuming, especially with multiple implementing agencies, and can be exacerbated by multiple sequencing being conducted in too short a time span. Its template, which limits discretionary response, may contribute to fostering a rigid "check the box" approach that limits added value. Risks identified are not weighted or prioritized and can lead to misleading "averages" or risk in situations where a small number of high risks dominates overall project risk. Although P-RAMS has a facility for procurement staff to override automatic ratings, there is little evidence that it is exercised. The P-RAMS template could also further sharpen its focus on fraud and corruption by featuring that risk as an additional risk factor.

In terms of results—that is, whether there is better risk management—evidence is limited on the value added of P-RAMS compared to previous project-level risk assessments. IEG compared procurement risk management before and after its introduction. A key finding is that procurement risk was already being managed to a generally high standard. Based on IEG's sample, it does not appear that the correlation between risk identification and risk mitigation has been much improved. There is also little evidence of sequenced decline in P-RAMS' residual risk, which raises questions about how risk mitigation measures are applied.

Another Bank instrument to guard against procurement risk is the tracking of misprocurement and procurement complaints, as well as preventive and investigative work undertaken by INT. Misprocurement rates represent 3–3.5 cases per thousand, which is low.

The Bank also maintains a central database of complaints made by bidders (mostly losing bidders) in relation to contract awards. Though the number of complaints has shown little variation over the past decade, an issue is their potential to impose delays in the procurement process. The average time for resolution of complaints has been about 150 days, but a significant number have taken much longer to resolve (Figure 6).

INT also has a role in monitoring procurement risk. It maintains information on suppliers that task teams are required to consult prior to preparing short lists. Although the Bank's sanctions lists—the list of suspended firms and the list of debarred firms—are mandatory and, in the case of the debarment list, coordinated with other IFIs, INT also maintains a Company Risk Profile Database: a list of suppliers where complaints have been received and a case has been opened, although not concluded. Technically, such firms are not suspended or debarred

FIGURE 6 Time to Resolve Complaints

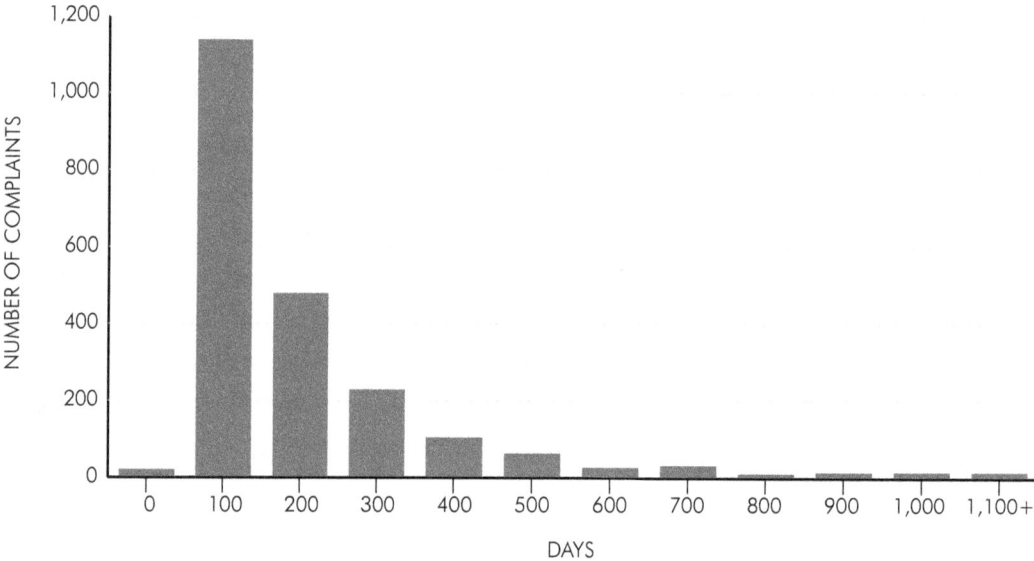

FIGURE 6 Time to Resolve Complaints

SOURCE: World Bank database.
NOTE: Based on 2,157 observations.

by the Bank, so task team leaders are not prohibited from approving contracts to suppliers in the database. However, they are advised to consult INT to get more insights. Apart from inevitable delays, this can provide ambiguous guidance to team leaders and country clients.

Procurement Tracking Systems

An important aspect of overall efficacy of the procurement process is the extent to which it makes efficient use of resources. Good management of the procurement process is needed to achieve good outcomes. IEG reviewed the extent to which the Bank is equipped to track its procurement transactions and their outcomes and found that current procurement tracking systems are not equipped to provide the information needed to monitor the achievement of procurement objectives of economy, efficiency, risk management, transparency, or value for money.

There is a rudimentary Bank-wide procurement tracking system that contains limited information on a subset of contracts. Three separate regional tracking systems have been developed in response to the lack of a central system, each with different objectives and architecture and its own merits and limitations. For those regions that do not have a tracking system, practices are diverse. Data are mostly maintained in field offices, and it is presently not possible to collect and analyze unified information on many basic procurement process parameters. Some of these limitations are well known, and at a Bank-wide level, efforts have been made to develop individual modules of a future system architecture. Today there is an agenda within the Operations Risk Management, Operations Policy and Country Services Vice Presidency to integrate aspects of these systems. Better tracking systems would enable closer monitoring of service standards and provide a first step, in conjunction with other measures, towards identifying and resolving procurement delays.

Yet blueprints fall considerably short of the Bank's potential. Properly harnessed, such information could not only help ensure that funds are used for intended purposes, but could also help the Bank make informed choices about markets and suppliers—for example, for setting methods thresholds and providing management information on the performance of the procurement process.

Such analyses could identify bottlenecks not only in procurement execution (elapsed times, clearance levels) but also in project execution (proportion of expenditures contracted/ disbursed) and agent execution (the client/borrower, task team leader, procurement specialists, and private contractors, if the system embraces contract management). Systems could also enable borrower/client monitoring of the procurement process and monitoring the extent to which core principles of procurement are observed: considerations of competition, economy, and efficiency; transparency and equity; and domestic market development.

Finally, such data could help increase global market transparency and price discovery—generating information for a wider group of market agents with the potential of getting better value for money not only for Bank projects but also for overall public sector efficiency in client countries and for other development agencies.

Analysis of Elapsed Time

Timeliness, process efficiencies, and delays in procurement have been raised as a prime concern by all participants in the procurement process. IEG's analysis of procurement process efficiency suggests that average time taken overall in the procurement process is long, and because of repeat iterations, much longer than Bank norms. A high level of variability in processing times exists, typically with a "long tail" of contracts that take considerably longer than average times (Figure 7). There is variation across procurement methods. NCB, even when prior reviewed, is notably quicker than ICB; conversely, consultant contract processing through quality and cost-based methods is particularly time consuming.

FIGURE 7 Time to Clear Contracts

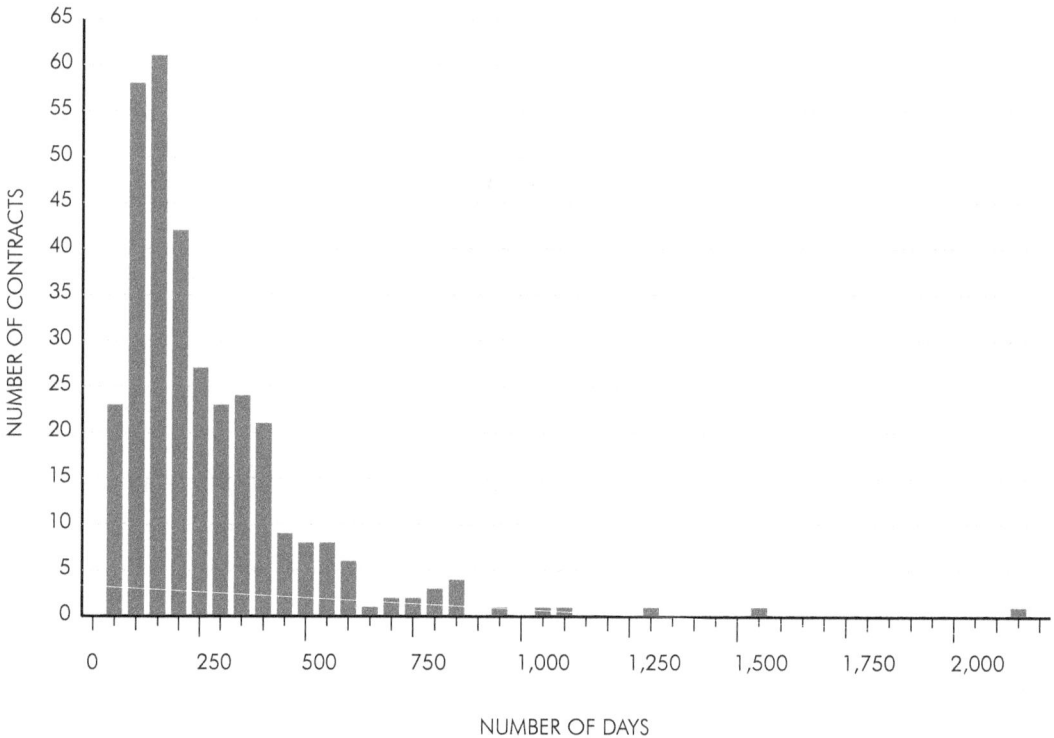

SOURCE: IEG analysis of a sample of contract data.

Analysis shows that the size of a contract is perhaps the single most important determinant of elapsed time. One factor could be the higher clearance thresholds for higher value projects. Data from the Africa Region show clearly that higher levels of clearance require considerably longer processing times. The analysis also suggests that country capacity and governance matter. Countries with lower Country Policy and Institutional Assessments—or International Development Association versus International Bank for Reconstruction and Development countries—require longer processing times.

New Modalities of Procurement

Looking ahead, new procurement methods such as framework agreements can offer a means toward increasing efficiency, for both the Bank and its clients. Many Bank client countries have introduced provisions for framework agreements in their own procurement systems. The Bank introduced the use of framework contracts from 2011 but limits their use, and in practice, they have been little used with Bank projects.

New procurement platforms, especially e-procurement, can offer considerable scope for improving procurement efficiencies, among other things also increasing transparency and lowering potential for corruption. Such platforms have won global advocacy and are being incorporated into new procurement legislation in major jurisdictions such as the European Union.

The Bank has been aware of the potential for e-procurement and has made efforts to include it in some of its technical assistance, but these efforts remain small in many countries because of limited resources and limited Bank familiarity. WBI's training courses partially compensate.

Going Forward

Clearly, much remains to be done to improve the quality of Bank support to client countries for building their own procurement systems and to improve the Bank's own procurement systems to increase the development impact of its lending. The Bank needs to retain a proactive leadership role in this area, in terms of introducing and encouraging best practice and also using its unique multicountry engagement to promote knowledge transfer and learning in the area of procurement.

BUILDING CAPACITY

Developing a strategic and long-term approach toward building procurement capacity in Bank client countries

Given the fragmented nature of support to building procurement capacity in Bank client countries, there is a need to develop a strategic and long-term approach toward building procurement capacity in these countries, integrated into CASs, and resourced to provide "hands-on" support for the present phase of capacity development, through vehicles such as technical assistance loans. At the country strategy level there is a need to refocus support to procurement from the emphasis on contract clearance toward country system and human capacity building.

As client countries' procurement systems mature and basic legal and institutional structures are put in place, there may be less scope for achieving change through policy-based loans. Going forward, the Bank may need to move from its present substantial focus on the DPL vehicle toward more hands-on technical assistance support.

Given the relatively small size of IDF grants, technical assistance loans that are grounded in predictable budgetary funding may provide more comprehensive, reliable, and longer-term support. Such loans will have to be built into country department work programs. In terms of content, country programs for procurement support could also enable better integration of procurement into the broader optic of public expenditure management.

Improving present diagnostic tools

The Bank, in parallel with other global partners, could support the fine tuning of the MAPS instrument, helping it fulfill its forward-looking mandate. Core elements of a revised MAPS would be an actionable set of compliance and performance indicators equipped to look at functional aspects of a procurement system and an integral action plan. Bank diagnostic work, meanwhile, could proceed with recent experiments that integrate the best features of the CPAR and MAPS, among other things, moving away from an emphasis on the legal systems and institutional frameworks and toward functional performance.

Efforts could also be made to better incorporate areas such as risk management, mechanisms for the detection and prevention of fraud and corruption, and complaints handling. Finally, better integration could be undertaken of procurement into the wider framework of public financial management and public sector expenditure.

Developing realistic, long-term programs for building human capacity in procurement

A starting point for such programs would be to determine the purpose of training, given the difference between hands-on support for implementing the Bank's lending program and building capacity for better country systems—recognizing, however, the place for the former in the whole. Benefit would be derived from looking at program features such as financial sustainability, attrition rates, incentives, and national recognition of procurement as a professional stream. Capacity building programs could also provide exposure to new global procurement modalities and global good practice.

However, it must also be recognized that building procurement capacity is an integral part of a wider civil service capacity building exercise, and it cannot be developed in isolation of the overall civil service cadre. Consideration could be given to Bank support for the integration of procurement into broader civil service training programs.

Supporting countries' own efforts to develop good procurement practices through better oversight

The Bank, through the WBI, has given some support to countries where independent external civil society organizations have made efforts to monitor public procurement. Today the sustainability of these efforts is not clear. Lending reinforcement to these efforts could help countries achieve greater self-sufficiency and independence in public procurement oversight.

ADAPTING BANK GUIDELINES TO NEW NEEDS

Fine tuning the current Guidelines

Although in broad terms Bank Guidelines remain serviceable and well adapted to traditional forms of lending, there is scope to consider fine tuning in a number of areas, such as the two-envelope system or bid response periods. There is also room for more fundamental review in aspects such as consultant hiring guidelines, including guidance on the choice of selection methods and types of contracts and on the preparation of consultant short lists (including regional constraints).

Beyond this, there is a need to review the provisions of the Bank's guidelines in terms of the treatment of new procurement modalities and instruments. The Bank could consider the expanded use of framework agreements and introduce, where appropriate, forms of negotiation beyond the Consultant Guidelines.

Undertaking specific revisions to present provisions for areas of complex procurement such as ICT and PPP

There is also a clear need for review of the present Guidelines in certain areas of complex procurement. IEG's suggestions are based on its review of two areas: ICT procurement and PPPs.

ICT Procurement

With regard to ICT procurement, despite recent progress, considerable further improvement could be made through measures such as streamlining Bank standard bidding documents for ICT and aligning them with best global practice. European Union Directives do not include standard bidding documents; however, the European Commission has developed some for its own use. The MDB heads of procurement have developed harmonized model documents for ICT procurement, but the Bank has not adopted them. These also need to be assessed.

The Bank could also consider offering opportunities for enhanced dialogue between bidders and procuring agents. The Bank's two-stage bidding process provides the opportunity for a dialogue to adjust technical requirements and commercial terms in the first stage, during evaluation of non-price technical proposals, but not in the second stage, during evaluation of price proposals. However, the review found that two-stage bidding is not frequently used for procurement of complex ICT systems because of perceptions that benefits do not outweigh the longer time involved. To enhance opportunities for dialogue, the Bank could review options for the adoption of competitive negotiation processes, similar to that of the European Union Directives and UNCITRAL model law, subject to borrower capacity. Additionally, greater use of direct negotiation with preferred suppliers (sole source) might be used less restrictively where circumstances warrant.

Smoother ICT procurement would be aided by better project design, including building consensus among stakeholders, more appropriate packaging of contracts, selective use of specialist consultants, and managing expectations. Disciplined contract implementation is also needed. Although it is not possible to freeze design in such systems, discipline is needed to stop adding features and functions as the system is implemented. Better—though selective—use of consultants is also a part of improved design and implementation, especially in agencies that are technically less competent, where further ICT procurement is not expected, or where the advisory role of the Bank can conflict with its oversight role.

At the same time, training and guidance in complex ICT procurement are needed for both procurement staff and task team leaders, so they better understand available flexibilities. At field staff levels, better incentive structures are needed to address the risk-averse culture. In parallel, there would be benefit from selectively reinforcing borrower capacity, especially in those ministries likely to implement such projects for a long period or those facing particular challenges in decentralized administrations.

Finally, IEG and Bank and country staff recognize that these problems are not unique to the Bank. Various studies show that contracts to supply ICT systems are difficult everywhere and corruption risks are high; some research reports that the success rate in large private sector information technology projects is about 50 percent.

PPP Procurement

The recent draft note of the Procurement Anchor of the Operations Policy and Country Services Vice Presidency on procurement policies for PPP projects would benefit from further clarification in several regards: (i) the scope of the Bank's review of private investor procedures and of standards acceptable to the Bank; (ii) situations where the Bank enters late and is not involved in the design (including the design of procurement processes) from the beginning; (iii) situations where the procurement arrangements have been put in place by other investors, sometimes with larger financial stakes, where the Bank might be a minority investor; (iv) on-lending arrangements, financing via investment funds, or other situations with numerous small investments under an umbrella arrangement; and (v) unsolicited proposals. In terms of on-lending, the Bank might consider methods to control downstream conflict of interest, such as through due diligence of the concession/subcontractor arrangements.

The Bank could make greater use of the International Financial Corporation model of adapting to country practices. Although it is unlikely that the Bank can take a purely private sector approach to PPPs, the International Finance Corporation (although very much like a private financier) must work within the PPP laws of the country and, at least for PPP projects, accept procurement policies that are somewhat public sector oriented. The Bank is seen as slow and ill equipped to adapt to the procedures of others, especially where quick response is needed, for example, to round out a financing consortium. One measure that would help address this is to give greater recognition to commercial confidentiality concerns that may make large players unwilling to share some information with a minor player, if considered commercially sensitive.

Greater clarity in standards would be beneficial. Regarding competitive procedures, arrangements that rely on "acceptability" and where deviations require "waivers" are opaque, and a simpler and more predictable process is preferable. Likewise, with regard to unsolicited proposals, the Bank's vaguely worded guidance says that this may need to be treated as an "exception" or that it may impose a competitive process. The Bank will need to balance the need for clearly articulated procedures that do not involve seeking exceptions with possible unintended consequences of greater specificity that could also be limiting.

In the same vein, the Bank could do more to develop model/standard documentation, such as standard concession agreements; provide clearer guidance on contract management; and provide more training for Bank staff engaged in PPP projects, recognizing their unique and case-by-case demands. Finally, the Bank could consider closer alignment with the practices of external agencies such as the European Union, in terms of selective use of negotiation to arrive at a PPP concession agreement.

Clarifying the form and content of proposed use of country systems and adopting a gradual approach

A first proposal is that the Bank will benefit from a review of the materiality of differences between the Bank and its client countries' systems, using a unified framework for all clients and the adoption of transparent standards on acceptable areas of flexibility. The Bank already follows a similar practice at a project level for NCB contracts. The system could be unified and expanded and used to adopt individually phased strategies toward incrementally greater use of country systems, in line with other MDBs.

IEG suggests that it may be early to make country-level decisions on whether to use country systems. Such a decision would presuppose uniform national methods and uniform capacity among implementing agencies, which does not exist. IEG also suggests that a contract-level approach would permit better alignment with capacity and with risk, as a part of the project procurement plan. This also builds on practices for NCB already in use at the Bank. As a track record is established, wider acceptance of country systems—for entire projects or for all projects undertaken by an implementing agency—could happen, with the eventual performance-based goal of approaching full use of country systems in some countries.

The decision to use country systems might be based not only on discussions with client governments, but also on the Bank's own risk assessments, taking into account the views of the private sector. The continued availability of Bank systems is presumed and may be preferred in some circumstances.

Finally, there is a need for greater clarification of the content and form of use of country systems, especially with regard to the extent to which they would also include Bank engagement, for example, in the procurement process, in fiduciary oversight, or in terms of legal recourse. Introducing greater Bank involvement in upstream and downstream procurement processes would also help provide greater assurance of the Bank's presence, although country procurement modalities would be used. There is also a need to provide assurance that there would be no change to the Bank's legal remedies and no change in existing rights and obligations concerning fraud and corruption.

Shifting the present approach to "prior review" and "methods" thresholds toward greater emphasis on risk as well as market information

Although present systems of risk management work with a reasonable level of effectiveness, there is scope for improvement in a number of areas. A first proposal is to reduce the present high reliance on the value-based prior review threshold system as a risk management tool and to adopt a risk-based approach, for example, through identification of risky contracts. It is also recommended that "methods" thresholds be constructed through better use of market information.

Streamlining other aspects of risk management: P-RAMS, Post-Procurement Reviews, and INT

The P-RAMS tool could be further refined to simplify the interface, ease the use of the "customize" and "override" features to permit realistic weighting of risk factors, set more realistic frequencies for P-RAMS sequences, improve the interface between P-RAMS and ORAF, and introduce a separate risk factor dealing with fraud and corruption risk. The Bank could periodically review the materiality of information collected and take appropriate follow-up action, moving P-RAMS away from being a compliance tool and toward being a substantive control element, not only for procurement risk but for overall project and portfolio risk.

The Bank could undertake more substantive Post-Procurement Reviews that recognize its potential as a risk management tool, beyond compliance with numeric quotas and toward an integration and review of their findings.

There would be benefit in considering further refinement to the role of INT with regard to procurement risk, in terms of reexamining present strategy on the use of the company risk profile database where INT cases are pending; strengthening the profiling of information on its complaints and cases; integrating these with the Bank's operational reporting systems; and tracking them on a regular basis.

The Bank could also more clearly define procurement and related risk concepts, including country risk, sector risk, project risk, procurement risk, and residual risk, and be sure these are consistently applied.

Finally, it is a given that any changes need to ensure integrity and transparency and present rights and obligations against the risk of fraud and corruption. However, fraud and corruption risk may be manifest at an overall systemic level. More Bank focus on the overall country level, perhaps as an element of country dialogue or strategy, in lieu of the present emphasis on the transactions level, could be more effective.

Integrated tracking systems and service standards

IEG supports recent Bank moves toward the integration of an information system and recommends that it be made a priority and expanded in scope. The present plans, however, fall short of an integrated Bank-wide procurement information system that covers managerial information, procurement planning, risk management, and efficiency parameters. Further modules will need to be developed to meet open data, benchmarking, and knowledge objectives. To assume a leadership and knowledge role in terms of good practice in procurement, it would be valuable if such a platform could be expanded to provide systematic information on markets, suppliers, and prices. These further elements are critical if economy, efficiency, and value for money are among the Bank's procurement objectives, and if the Bank plans to monitor their achievement.

IEG suggests that more systematic attention be paid to elapsed time in procurement, as part of the integrated Bank-wide platform. This would involve the setting and monitoring of service standards that are adapted to the relative risk of transactions and that are transparently monitored on a Bank-wide basis.

Adopting efficiency-increasing procurement methods and platforms

The Bank could consider increasing its support for the adoption of new procurement methods (such as framework agreements) and platforms (notably, e-procurement) that have the capacity to contribute to increased efficiency as well as transparency in procurement.

OTHER AREAS FOR STRENGTHENING DEVELOPMENT EFFECTIVENESS

The Bank should take into consideration the extent to which public procurement is influenced by other factors, such as the overall levels of competition, the nature of governance, and the investment climate. Finally, the Bank could also consider the extent to which the experience of other external players, including both donors and country clients, could be brought to bear on its present policy on domestic preferences, to the extent that this remains a guiding principle of Bank procurement policy. The Bank would benefit from further reviewing the integration of the concept of sustainability in procurement, better reflecting other operational practices in the Bank, as well as increasingly external practice among other development partners.

Recommendations

These findings point to the following recommendations to improve the effectiveness of the Bank's support to country procurement capacity building, as well as the effectiveness of procurement in Bank lending.

Review the need for support to procurement capacity within the context of all CASs. Where identified as a priority, adopt country-level strategic plans to build procurement capacity in client countries that make specific resource commitments for this objective, integrated within the context of civil service reform, planning and budgeting, and economic management.

Embedding support to procurement capacity building within the country strategy framework, and subject to its monitoring indicators, would address fragmented support to building procurement capacity, enable the development of a long-term approach, and provide necessary resources to move toward hands-on technical support and away from the present substantial focus on DPLs.

Procurement reform is constrained at the country level by overall civil service capacity. And there is a need to integrate the development of such capacity within the wider context of county-level financial and economic management.

Adopt revisions to procurement diagnostic frameworks, specifically the review and revision of diagnostic tools (MAPS, CPARs, and the procurement-related elements of PEFA).

During the period of mandatory CPARs, there was more systematic attention to the issue of procurement in country strategies. CPAR guidelines addressed areas intended for Bank country dialogue, notably pointing out differences relative to the Bank, as required for project lending, incorporating flexibility to address country-specific issues and including action plans for improving procurement.

Although CPARs sometimes had scattered treatment of subjects, MAPS assessments benefited from their rigid framework as a tool for benchmarking and comparison. Yet they have also had limitations, in terms of tracking reform progress over time, partly reflecting the limited use of MAPS compliance and performance indicators, in view of their complexity.

Agree on clearly defined responsibilities for sector specialists/technical experts, task team leaders, and procurement staff in contract management. Implement defined responsibilities.

In terms of procurement implementation, the role of procurement staff has sometimes taken the place of sector technical specialists, a role that they cannot be expected to cover. There is also ambiguity regarding the role of the task team leader. Clarification of these respective obligations per project would ensure that procurement, specifically, would receive adequate resources.

Revise and implement changes in the current Bank Guidelines, including new procurement modalities, the consultant hiring guidelines, and areas of the Guidelines and standard bidding documents referring to ICT and PPP, taking account of IEG's findings and reflective of prevailing good practice.

Although Bank Guidelines remain serviceable and well adapted to traditional forms of lending, there is scope for fine tuning in a number of areas and for more fundamental review of consultant hiring guidelines; expanded use of new modalities of procurement, such as framework agreements and forms of negotiation; and clarification and amendment of Guidelines, as well as standard bidding documents in areas of complex procurement, especially ICT and PPP procurement. When revisions are made, care should be taken to guard against the unintended consequence of making the Guidelines more inflexible.

Adopt a progressive approach toward the greater use of country systems, based first on the materiality of differences between Bank and country systems, and second on country, agency, and private sector capacity. The Bank could approve subcomponents of a system, such as specific contracts, categories, methods, or specific administrative entities. Clarify, where used, the form and content of the proposed use of country systems, in terms of Bank oversight and recourse.

In line with other MDBs, the Bank could adopt a more pragmatic approach toward the use of country systems, which will permit a progressive move toward this goal, beginning with individual contracts, based on specific categories or methods of procurement, specific projects, or implementing agencies, depending on client capacity both in the government and the private sector.

Focus resources on high-risk contracts for prior review, reducing emphasis on value thresholds. Improve the use of risk-monitoring tools and risk-mitigation methods, through the analysis of risk data from P-RAMs and Post-Procurement Reviews, for example, by clustering to draw out patterns and trends and streamlining details of the P-RAMS instrument.

Reducing the present reliance on the value-based prior review threshold system as a risk management tool with a risk-based approach, for example, through identification of risky contracts, would enable more effective use of procurement resources, as would better use of market information for the construction of "methods" thresholds. P-RAMS could be improved in terms of its interface, frequency, and links to other operational risk management systems. The Bank could conduct more substantive post procurement reviews that recognize their potential as a risk management tool.

Enhance and integrate Bank-wide procurement information and tracking systems in areas that include procurement planning and implementation, time taken for specific steps of the procurement process, and risk identification and mitigation. Implement and monitor service standards for turnaround of procurement transactions on a homogenous Bank-wide basis.

IEG supports recent Bank moves toward the integration of some procurement information systems and recommends that this be made a priority and expanded in scope to cover managerial information, procurement planning, risk management, and efficiency parameters. Further modules will need to be developed to meet open data, benchmarking, and knowledge objectives. In parallel, service standards for elapsed time in procurement could be monitored through the integrated Bank-wide platform. This would involve the setting and monitoring of service standards that are adapted to the relative risk of transactions and that are transparently monitored on a Bank-wide basis.

Management Response | INTRODUCTION

Management welcomes the Independent Evaluation Group's (IEG) report *The World Bank and Public Procurement: An Independent Evaluation* and commends IEG for the scope and questions raised as part of the evaluation. The release of the report comes at an important time, as the World Bank plans to move forward with its proposed new framework for procurement in World Bank investment project finance. Critically, the IEG report supports the need to update the Bank's procurement policies and procedures. IEG's findings are informative and will further assist management in its proposed development of operational procurement policies and procedures. While work is ongoing to update the procurement policies and procedures, management will also ensure that the existing scope for procurement innovation is emphasized and supported under current policy.

The IEG report collects considerable information, using a comprehensive methodology, in relation to two overarching questions:

- The extent to which the Bank has helped its clients to develop better procurement capacity and improve their public procurement systems; and

- The extent to which application of the Bank's existing procurement guidelines has helped support the Bank's own development effectiveness objectives, in terms of fostering economy, efficiency and transparency in the execution of Bank-supported, Bank-financed projects in client countries.

The IEG evaluation finds that on the whole, country clients, the private sector, and Bank staff agree that the Bank's present procurement guidelines are successful in certain aspects—securing fairness, competition, and transparency in procurement for Bank-financed projects. It also identifies scope for improvement, in particular to reflect new modalities of modern procurement practice. In addition, the evaluation finds that there is less comfort with Bank procurement processes, for example, with regard to time taken, adaptability, effort expended on low value contracts, and consistency. The bulk of Bank procurement budgetary resources has gone to support transactional activities, while limited resources have been available to support procurement capacity building, which experienced a decline from 2007 after diagnostic updates were no longer mandatory. This has resulted in fragmented support to procurement training and capacity building in client countries. When the Bank has been able to support institutional strengthening in client countries, leveraging its experience in operational procurement to support procurement reforms, there have been significant successes. Overall, the report concludes that the Bank has played a lead role in advancing the global agenda of building and harmonizing good practice in public procurement and this work has been widely recognized by development partners and client countries alike.

Management General Comments
FINDINGS FROM MANAGEMENT'S GLOBAL CONSULTATIONS

In April 2012, the Board of Executive Directors and senior management agreed to undertake a further review of the Bank's procurement policies and procedures. As part of this review process, between May 2012 and February 2013, the Bank held consultations across 96 countries, with about 2,000 stakeholders from client and donor governments, the private sector, civil society, academia, and other development partners. Stakeholders identified a range of challenges to the existing policy and procedures, and the main messages were as follows:

• The need for a robust set of principles, reflecting *new concepts in public procurement* and stressing the overarching importance of supporting development effectiveness, value for money, integrity, and sustainability.

• The *need for procurement methods* that are context specific, proportional, and best fit for purpose, that allow for innovation, and that *reflect modern, international good practice.*

• The *greater use of country systems, with appropriate arrangements to manage associated risks* throughout the whole project cycle, including in regard to Bank monitoring of contract execution, as well as recourse to the Bank and dispute resolution.

• Accompanying the use of country systems with more *support for capacity building, especially in lower-income countries,* and across all the actors—private business, nongovernmental organizations, civil society, and public institutions.

• The *deployment of e-procurement and other technologies* with attendant benefits in terms of time, cost, and transparency. This can reduce the potential for fraud and corruption and allow data mining and analysis.

- *Special attention to fragile and conflict-affected situations and small economies* with poorly developed markets, weak capacity, and limited options for economies of scale and competition.

- A *strategic approach* informed by upfront analysis of markets, industry practices, and competition, including the impact on local industry.

- *Coverage of the full procurement cycle*, from design through planning, tendering, contract execution, and completion. This would balance compliance with specific rules during the tendering process, with more attention to quality, results, and performance.

- *New thinking about the Bank's approach to fraud and corruption*, taking a holistic stance, looking at contract execution as well as tendering, integrating with local accountability institutions, and using new technologies and transparency initiatives.

- *Renewed international partnerships* with standard-setters, multilateral development banks and donors, and other relevant global organizations.

- *Clarification of the Bank's role* with respect to that of borrowers and development partners, as well as clarification of roles internally in the Bank.

- Bank's direct oversight of procurement processes *focusing on the largest and most complex and innovative contracts*, and indirect oversight increasingly relying on country systems as well as civil society and independent observers.

- *Metrics to measure results* on the ground, changes to borrower/country capacity and professionalism, and the contribution of the Bank.

Management sees a great deal of synergy between IEG's recommendations and the issues identified during its global consultations, noted above. The IEG recommendations are focused primarily on improving implementation and ensuring that the guidelines reflect new procurement modalities and prevailing good practice. Stakeholders in the global consultations raised additional issues, with a call for Bank procurement to be more principles based, proportional, and fit for purpose. The broad issues identified are similar, and the call for change and modernization is consistent. Taken together, the IEG report and the key messages from management's own consultation provide a positive platform for updating the procurement policies and procedures. The IEG report confirms that effective procurement is critical to the Bank's operational work and underscores the need to adapt procurement policies and procedures to respond to new challenges and modalities.

The IEG report emphasizes the need to focus resources on higher risk/higher value activities and reduce the review of lower value contracts. Management agrees that a fit for purpose and proportional approach needs to be applied. The evaluation also helpfully provides specific advice on the prior review process (that is, review prior to contract signing) as follows:

- There is likely scope to reduce the share of contracts that are prior reviewed, focusing prior reviews on the highest risk contracts. This reflects the view that current prior review thresholds could be raised with beneficial impacts on workload and clearance time, and with only limited impact on risk or competition. IEG findings show that prior review instruments at best partially reflect country or project risk, and as such, could be relied on less as risk control mechanisms.

- Any additional risk that could arise from a reduction in the number of prior reviews could be mitigated by better use of Post-Procurement Reviews and independent procurement reviews. This need not imply an increase in their numbers, but rather a more strategic use of their findings.

Management's analysis of prior reviews in FY13 shows that Bank staff prior-reviewed 8,082 contracts, accounting for $9.4 billion of activity. The trigger for a prior review is based on a combination of risk/value, market conditions, and/or where the contract has been subject to international competitive bidding (ICB). As such, prior review of lower-value contracts can be warranted in high-risk environments or complex markets. However, 80 percent of prior reviews undertaken (by volume) account for 6 percent of the total value of these contracts—see Table 1 for a summary of prior reviews undertaken in FY13.

The data in Table 1 show that there is scope to apply a more fit for purpose and proportional approach to prior reviews, focusing resources on the highest risk and highest value contracts, reducing the review of lower value and/or lower risk contracts. Changing this focus would release resources to increase support for higher added value activities such as contract management and the strengthening of client procurement arrangements and institutions. This recommendation to focus effort on higher value/more strategic work has been corroborated by stakeholders during management's consultations.

TABLE 1 Summary Analysis of Prior Reviews in FY13

Prior Review Contract Type	Total Value	Number of Contracts	Mean Value of Each Prior Review	Median Value of Each Prior Review
Civil Works	$6,150,981,752	1,051	$5,853,897	$698,815
Goods and Services (nonconsulting)	$1,843,997,225	1,885	$978,300	$181,508
Consultants	$1,371,139,425	5,146	$266,448	$35,367
TOTAL	$9,366,118,401	8,082	$7,098,644	$915,690

SOURCE: World Bank data.
NOTE: Bank staff members and/or consultants review another 10,000 contracts (approximate) on an ex post sampled basis; typically these contracts are not ICB and are low value.

REVISE AND MODERNIZE THE GUIDELINES

The IEG report highlights the need to update, modernize, and implement changes to the current guidelines. Management agrees and proposes to update the guidelines focusing on guiding principles of economy, efficiency, effectiveness, integrity, fairness, openness, and transparency—as well as to reflect new modalities of procurement. This will help meet the diverse needs of clients as well as respond to a global economy that is calling for more up-to-date, modern, and innovative forms of procurement that can better contribute to results and value for money. Further, the IEG report also touches on specific issues, such as PPPs, community-driven development, two-envelope systems, framework agreements, eco-labeling and environmental laws, and difficulties in cofinancing. This analysis has reconfirmed a need to address these and other issues as we update the guidelines and procedures. To deliver this, management envisages that the current guidelines, as they now stand, would be replaced by (i) a statement of the need to fulfill the core principles, reflected in a new operational policy; (ii) a description of procedures to be followed by staff, reflected in a new statement of Bank procedures; and (iii) a tool box of methods, procedures, processes, standard bidding documents, templates, and supporting documentation to serve as guidance to staff and borrowers. These guidance materials would constitute the reference point in terms of the best that the Bank has to offer and would be continuously updated.

To empower the use of best practice and new modalities, management is of the view that the tool box of methods, procedures, and processes should become one of several different fit for purpose procurement approaches acceptable to the Bank, recognizing that the final call on the appropriateness of any procurement system rests with the Bank as part of its fiduciary assurance role. In the meantime, management will also ensure that the existing scope for procurement innovation and efficiency gains are emphasized and supported under current policy. This recommendation (to modernize the Bank's guidelines) has also been corroborated by stakeholders during management's consultations, with further calls made for a robust set of principles, reflecting new concepts in public procurement and stressing the overarching importance of supporting development effectiveness, value for money, integrity, and sustainability; and procurement methods that are context specific, proportional, and best fit for purpose, that allow for innovation, and that reflect modern, international good practice.

PROGRESSIVE USE OF CLIENT PROCUREMENT ARRANGEMENTS AND INSTITUTIONS

Management agrees that capacity development and retention are critical elements in enabling use of client procurement arrangements and institutions. A progressive use of client arrangements would involve the Bank adopting a sequenced strategy to identify opportunities to utilize alternate procurement arrangements, in whole or in part, to support Bank operations. Alternate procurement arrangements could include those of the European Union, other multilateral development banks where the World Bank is a minority financier, or a client's own procurement arrangements. Critically, the decision on the most appropriate procurement arrangements to utilize in a Bank operation should be proportional and fit for purpose. Management's view is that where a borrower requests to use its own procurement arrangements and institutions in a particular Bank operation, the overall standard of procurement performance required by the Bank will be no less than present, implying that the Bank could agree if the arrangements are satisfactory, or conditionally agree, insisting on a concrete and monitored action plan, or require the use of the guidelines if the arrangements are less than satisfactory. The recommendation to utilize different, fit for purpose procurement arrangements including those of clients has been corroborated by stakeholders during management's consultations. Management will develop proposals as part of its envisaged new framework for procurement in World Bank investment project finance.

Management agrees with IEG that performance of the procurement function depends not only on the procurement network within the Bank, but also on the collaboration and input of other networks and regional units across the institution. This reflects the synergies that exist in client countries especially when it comes to strengthening institutions, which in turn depend on the governance structures, the efficiency of the country's public service, the investment climate, and so on. IEG has identified a lack of clarity on the extent of support to be provided during the contract management phase and whether this should be provided by Bank procurement staff, Bank task team leaders, technical experts, or national institutions. The existing role and approach to contract management will be examined and addressed, in particular examining the legal implications versus the potential operational benefits. This recommendation for clarity of roles and in particular the approach to contract management has also been corroborated by stakeholders during management's consultations.

IEG's Recommendations

Management agrees with the key recommendations in the IEG report, such as revising the guidelines to reflect new modalities for procurement, strengthening diagnostic and monitoring tools, more technical assistance that is adequately resourced, more focus on higher risk/value activities, and less focus on low value or low risk contracts. IEG's report and the Bank's own policy reform consultations both emphasize the crucial and exemplary role of Bank procurement, but also point out the need for strategic capacity building and modernization, emphasizing value for money, integrity, and a controlled push for using client procurement arrangements and institutions when appropriate. Taken together, IEG's specific recommendations and stakeholders' advice on policy reform identify the need for change and provide a comprehensive picture for management to take forward the proposed new framework for procurement in World Bank investment project finance. This proposed new framework will address a wide range of issues that will set the path for Bank procurement to further clients' development goals even more strongly in the future. Management will be engaging further with the Board (Committee on Development Effectiveness and Audit Committee) on its change program for procurement in the coming months.

Management Action Record

Country-Level Focus
IEG FINDINGS AND CONCLUSIONS

Good public procurement practices are a major determinant of the effectiveness of public expenditure. On behalf of their citizens, governments typically spend as much as between 5 and 20 percent of their gross domestic product on procurement of goods and services, and effective procurement policies enable better use of government budgets. Good national procurement practices are therefore an essential element of the poverty reduction focus of the Bank. Equally, sound public procurement in client countries is a prerequisite for the success of the Bank's newly introduced Program for Results lending instrument, which uses national procurement policies, and may allow procurement practices in Bank lending to be unified across investment and policy-based lending, and harmonized with other donors.

IEG findings show that there has been an absence of strategic planning for procurement capacity building, and these efforts have been fragmented. There has been a loose translation of priorities, from procurement discussions in country strategies to specific actions, in the country work program for procurement reform. Attention in early years focused on diagnostic work, and there was limited effort to find vehicles that would provide hands-on support with implementation of diagnostic findings and build them into the work program. Support for capacity building has been fragmented, with an excessive reliance on development policy loans. As client countries' procurement systems mature and basic legal and institutional structures are put in place, there is less scope for achieving change through policy-based loans, with more need for hands-on support through technical assistance. Given the relatively small size of institutional development fund grants, technical assistance loans that are better grounded in predictable budgetary funding may provide more comprehensive, reliable, and longer-term support.

Reviews of procurement, viewed through the public finance lens of the Public Expenditure and Financial Accountability (PEFA) instrument, do not suggest a close integration of procurement within the public expenditure management framework. Moreover, there was little attention to public sector management issues such as cash planning or commitment reporting.

Limited success achieved in procurement capacity building is due to endemic country issues as much as to Bank-related issues. Although the Bank attempted some procurement capacity building in most countries, it was mostly with a focus on immediate needs for implementing Bank lending. On the government side, resources are invariably stretched, civil service salaries are low, and staff turnover is typical. The lack of recognition of procurement as a professional stream is an impediment that some governments have tried to address. However, building procurement capacity is also an integral part of a wider civil service capacity-building exercise, and it cannot be developed in isolation of the overall civil service cadre.

IEG RECOMMENDATIONS

Review the need for support to procurement capacity within the context of all Country Assistance Strategies. Where they have been identified as a priority, adopt country-level strategic plans to build procurement capacity in client countries that make specific resource commitments for this objective, integrated within the context of civil service reform, planning and budgeting, and economic management.

ACCEPTANCE BY MANAGEMENT

World Bank: Agree

MANAGEMENT RESPONSE

Management agrees that decisions on how to support procurement in each country should be taken in the first instance in the context of the Bank's country engagement strategy in the country concerned. This issue has been identified in the proposed new framework for procurement in World Bank investment project finance. It is envisaged that when the Country Partnership Framework (including the lending program) is determined, the procurement profile, including opportunities and risks, can be assessed. The procurement profile for a country would be informed by a diagnostic of the sectors in which engagement is planned, the broad market conditions (competitiveness, price trends, innovations, and so forth) in those sectors, the institutions likely to be involved in implementation, and their procurement arrangements. This diagnostic exercise would incorporate an understanding of the sectors in which engagement is planned, the broad market conditions (competitiveness, price trends, innovations, and so forth) in those sectors, the institutions likely to be involved in implementation, and their procurement arrangements. This assessment would identify the appropriate procurement approach in each instrument, including opportunities to utilize client procurement arrangements and institutions, with recommendations for procurement capacity building as appropriate within the context of public service reforms.

Final decisions on resource commitments will need to be taken in the context of competing development objectives and priorities of the country.

Diagnostic Frameworks and Tools

IEG FINDINGS AND CONCLUSIONS

During the period of mandatory Country Procurement Assessment Reports (CPARs), there was more systematic attention to the issue of procurement in country strategies. CPAR guidelines addressed areas intended for Bank country dialogue, notably pointing out differences relative to the Bank, as required for project lending, and incorporating flexibility to address country-specific issues, and including action plans for improving procurement. Yet CPARs sometimes had scattered treatment of subjects.

Although Methodology for Assessing Procurement Systems (MAPS) exercises had a more consistent structure, they were deemed to provide a "snapshot" of the system, rather than a roadmap for reform. Their limitations in terms of describing the functioning of a procurement system partly reflect the limited use of the MAPS performance indicators—possibly reflecting their complexity in environments of limited data availability. The recent integration of MAPS into CPARs in some countries is perhaps the most useful diagnostic tool, acknowledging the positive features of each. MAPS assessments benefited from their rigid framework as a tool for benchmarking and comparison. Yet they have also had limitations, in terms of tracking reform progress over time, partly reflecting the limited use of MAPS compliance and performance indicators, in view of their complexity.

IEG RECOMMENDATIONS

Adopt revisions to procurement diagnostic frameworks, specifically the review and revision of diagnostic tools (MAPS, CPARs, and procurement-related elements of PEFAs).

ACCEPTANCE BY MANAGEMENT

World Bank: Agree

The diagnostic framework will be revised in the context of the proposed new framework for procurement in World Bank investment project finance. The Bank is engaged with the Organisation for Economic Co-Operation and Development on a review of the MAPS methodology and will seek to positively influence its development. Similarly the Bank is also working closely with the PEFA secretariat to enhance the PEFA framework for better measurement of country systems. Internally, management will review and revise the procurement diagnostic framework, ensuring that the assessment leads to reforms that are sustainable and seek to obtain value for money.

Staff Roles and Responsibilities

IEG FINDINGS AND CONCLUSIONS

It is not clear whether or to what extent support (during the contract management phase) should be provided by Bank procurement staff, Bank task team leaders, technical experts, or national institutions that can provide support, whether hands on (project implementation agencies) or through oversight functions (such as a national audit office). In Bangladesh, for example, procurement staff felt that more engagement with contract management represents an oversight and advisory function for national execution, rather than a transfer of responsibility to the Bank. Among Bank staff, there is a need to review and resolve limitations in the present incentive structure, experience, and turnover of task team leaders. The role and extent of the Bank's procurement function will need to be considered relative to the roles of other agents in the country.

The role of procurement staff has sometimes taken the place of sector technical specialists, a role that they cannot be expected to cover. There is also ambiguity regarding the role of the task team leader. Clarification of these respective obligations per project would ensure that procurement, specifically, would receive adequate resources.

IEG RECOMMENDATIONS

Agree on clearly defined responsibilities for sector specialists/technical experts, task team leaders, and procurement staff in contract management. Implement defined responsibilities.

ACCEPTANCE BY MANAGEMENT

World Bank: Partially Agree

The Bank's procurement policy does not currently include a role for procurement in contract management. BP 11.0 states that the sector (task team leader) is responsible for reviewing or arranging for a technical expert to review the technical aspects of the projects and their related contracts. The role of the procurement specialist is currently limited to procurement reviews. However, it is agreed that the procurement specialist role needs to be more clearly defined. A comprehensive review of Bank roles and responsibilities in contract management will be undertaken. This will inform procurement development activities within the proposed new framework for procurement in World Bank investment project finance. This review will also involve consideration of both the operational and legal aspects of Bank involvement, as well as the opportunities that may be present to support greater development effectiveness in projects.

Changes to the Current Procurement Guidelines

IEG FINDINGS AND CONCLUSIONS

Findings show scope for fundamental review in aspects of the consultant hiring guidelines, where there was evidence of concern in areas including the choice of selection methods and preparation of consultant short lists. Bank Guidelines are also limited in terms of their incorporation of new modalities for procurement, such as framework agreements and use of negotiation. As regards information and communications technology (ICT) procurement, the evaluation notes that the Bank's standard bidding documents are not user friendly and are not aligned with industry norms. The Bank offers limited scope for dialogue between bidders and procuring agents. The Bank's two-stage bidding procedure provides the opportunity for a dialogue to adjust technical requirements and commercial terms in the first stage, during evaluation of nonpriced technical proposals, but not in the second stage, during evaluation of price proposals. Moreover, two-stage bidding is not frequently used for procurement of complex ICT systems. As regards public-private partnership (PPP) procurement, there is a need to further clarify (i) the scope of the Bank's review of private investor procedures and of standards acceptable to the Bank; (ii) situations where the Bank enters late and is not involved in the design (including the design of procurement processes) from the beginning; (iii) situations where the procurement arrangements have been put in place by other investors, sometimes with larger financial stakes, where the Bank might be a minority investor; (iv) on-lending arrangements, financing via investment funds, or other situations with numerous small investments under an umbrella arrangement; and (v) unsolicited proposals.

IEG RECOMMENDATIONS

Revise and implement changes in the current guidelines, including particularly new procurement modalities, the consultant hiring guidelines, and areas of the guidelines and standard bidding documents referring to ICT and PPP, taking account of IEG's findings and reflective of prevailing good practice.

World Bank: Agree

The guidelines will be reviewed and updated to reflect new procurement modalities. As part of its proposed new framework for procurement in World Bank investment project finance, management envisages that the World Bank procurement guidelines would become one of several different procurement arrangements that could be utilized to support a Bank operation.

Management envisages that the current guidelines, as they now stand, would be replaced by (i) a statement of the need to fulfill the core principles, reflected in a new operational policy; (ii) a description of procedures to be followed by staff, reflected in a new statement of Bank procedures; and (iii) a tool box of methods, procedures, processes, standard bidding documents, templates, and supporting documentation to serve as guidance to staff and borrowers. These guidance materials would constitute the reference point in terms of the best that the Bank has to offer and would be continuously updated.

This approach would empower the procurement team to exercise discretion to identify the most proportional, fit for purpose procurement arrangements, reflective of prevailing good practice and our procurement principles to support a Bank project. The final decision on the appropriateness of any alternate procurement arrangements to support individual operations will rest with the Bank (procurement) as part of its obligation to provide fiduciary assurance. Standard bidding documents will also be reviewed and changes will be identified to take account of IEG's findings.

Use of Country Systems
IEG FINDINGS AND CONCLUSIONS

The Bank developed its own pilot approach toward the use of country systems, an effort characterized by rigor but also minutiae in terms of detailed specification of necessary areas of compliance or conformity to the Bank needed. While most country systems have some differences from the Bank, some differences have greater materiality than others, in terms of underlying Bank principles, touching on core principles of promoting competition and market access; others impact less on such principles and there may be scope for flexibility. IEG also found mixed views between country clients and private suppliers that reflect ambiguity in the concept of "use of country systems," which would benefit from clarification, especially with regard to the extent to which they would also include, for example, Bank engagement in the procurement process, in fiduciary oversight, or in terms of legal recourse.

The Inter-American Development Bank and proposed African Development Bank use of country systems programs contrast with the Bank's pilot, which strove for full compliance to a set of criteria for the full range of procurement circumstances, including international competitive bidding (except consultant recruitment). The Bank's general intention was to approve national systems for use on all projects in a country. The Inter-American Development Bank and African Development Bank are attempting to avoid the "all or nothing" approach, striving to gradually move to full use of country systems though a measured process involving partial use, conditional acceptance, agreed improvements, and considerations of intent and objectives.

IEG RECOMMENDATIONS

Adopt a progressive approach toward greater use of country systems, based first on the materiality of differences between Bank and country systems and second on country, agency, and private sector capacity. The Bank could approve subcomponents of a system, such as specific contracts, categories, methods, or administrative entities. Clarify, where used, the form and content of the use of country systems proposed, in terms of Bank oversight and recourse.

ACCEPTANCE BY MANAGEMENT

World Bank: Agree

MANAGEMENT RESPONSE

Management agrees on the need to adopt a progressive approach to utilize client procurement arrangements and institutions in whole or in part, as appropriate. Critically, the decision on the most appropriate procurement arrangements to utilize in a Bank operation should be proportional and fit for purpose, with the final decision resting with the Bank (procurement team) as part of its obligation to provide fiduciary assurance.

Management has made proposals to update its approach to operational procurement, with an increased focus on strengthening client procurement arrangements and institutions as an integral part of its proposed new framework for procurement in World Bank investment project finance. If agreed, this approach envisages the World Bank procurement guidelines becoming one of several different procurement arrangements that could be utilized to support a Bank operation. Response [to previous recommendation] above.

Risk Control and Mitigation
IEG FINDINGS AND CONCLUSIONS

The Bank puts considerable emphasis, in terms of its present risk management framework, on ex ante risk controls through mechanisms such as prior review and clearance thresholds, which require contracts above certain values to be prior reviewed by procurement staff at increasing levels of seniority, depending on contract value. Yet findings show that prior review instruments at best partially reflect country or project risk, and as such, could be relied on less as risk control mechanisms. There is likely to be scope to reduce the risk efficiency trade-off by reducing the share of contracts that are prior reviewed and focusing prior review on the highest risk contracts. Bank procurement staff acknowledges that current review procedures are helpful for controlling fiduciary risk. Nevertheless, on balance, there is a view that current prior review threshold could be raised with beneficial impacts on workload and clearance time, and only limited impact on risk or competition.

Additional risk that this may imply could be mitigated by better use of Post-Procurement Reviews and independent procurement reviews. This need not imply an increase in their numbers, but rather a more strategic use of their findings. There is limited analysis of the effectiveness or outcomes of pivotal risk management tools such as the procurement threshold system, the content of Post-Procurement Reviews, or data collected through the most recent tool, the Procurement Risk Assessment Management System (P-RAMS) instrument, in terms of analyzing content, tracing trends, or correlating risk management and procurement outcomes.

The P-RAMS template and process can be cumbersome and time consuming, especially with multiple implementing agencies, and exacerbated by multiple sequencing being conducted in far too short a time span. Its template, which limits discretionary response, may contribute to fostering a rigid "check the box" approach which limits added value. Risks identified are not weighted or prioritized and can lead to misleading "averages" or risk in situations where a small number of high risks dominate overall project risk. While the P-RAMS system has a facility for procurement staff to override automatic ratings, it is not transparent and there is little evidence that it is exercised. The P-RAMS template could also further sharpen its focus on fraud and corruption by featuring fraud and corruption risk as an additional risk factor.

Focus resources on high-risk contracts for prior review, reducing emphasis on value thresholds. Improve the use of risk monitoring tools and risk mitigation methods, through the analysis of risk data from P-RAMs and Post-Procurement Reviews, for example, by clustering to draw out patterns and trends; and through streamlining details of the P-RAMs instrument.

ACCEPTANCE BY MANAGEMENT

World Bank: Partially Agree

MANAGEMENT RESPONSE

The prior reviews are not based on value thresholds only. The approach is a combination of risk and value. However, management agrees that more focus needs to be placed on higher risk/higher value activities, reducing the review of lower value and/or lower risk contracts. In practice, this will mean reducing the number of prior reviews of lower value and/or lower risk contracts, as such, increasing the Bank's risk exposure in these areas. However, management agrees with IEG that this will have "only limited impact on risk and competition"—in FY13, 80 percent of prior reviews undertaken (by volume) account for 6 percent of the total value of these contracts. Management proposes to update its approach to prior reviews, reflecting IEG's findings, releasing resources so they can focus more effort on the highest risk and/or highest value contracts.

Management agrees with IEG that the institutional system to manage procurement risks can be sharpened in focus, better integrated with other systems, and better used in terms of data input and analysis of findings.

P-RAMS can be simplified and more guidance to staff on how to use the tool can be provided. Reporting tools can be built to address analytical needs. Fraud and corruption dimensions of risks can also be more explicit within the P-RAMS tool. Decisions on the timing of information system changes will need to be taken in the context of evolving fiscal priorities.

Information and Tracking Systems

IEG FINDINGS AND CONCLUSIONS

IEG reviewed the extent to which the Bank is equipped to track its procurement transactions and their outcomes and finds that current procurement tracking systems are not equipped to provide key information needed to monitor the achievement of procurement objectives of economy, efficiency, risk management, transparency or value for money. There is a rudimentary Bank-wide procurement tracking system that contains limited information on a subset of contracts. Three separate regional "tracking" systems have been developed, in response to the lack of a central system, each with different objectives and architecture and its own merits and limitations. For those regions that do not have a tracking system, practices are diverse. Data are mostly maintained in field offices and it is presently not possible to collect and analyze unified information on many basic procurement process parameters. At a Bank-wide level, efforts have been made to develop individual modules of future system architecture. There is an agenda within Operations Risk Management to integrate aspects of these systems. Yet present blueprints fall considerably short of the Bank's potential. Properly harnessed, such information could not only help ensure that funds are used for intended purposes, but could help the Bank make informed choices about markets and suppliers and provide management information on the performance of the procurement process. Finally, such data could help increase global market transparency and price discovery—generating information for a wider group of market agents with the potential of getting better value for money not only for Bank projects but also for overall public sector efficiency in client countries, and for other agencies of development.

IEG RECOMMENDATIONS

Enhance and integrate Bank-wide procurement information and tracking systems, in areas that include procurement planning and implementation, time taken at specific steps of the procurement process, and risk identification and mitigation.

Implement and monitor service standards for turnaround of procurement transactions on a homogenous Bank-wide basis.

ACCEPTANCE BY MANAGEMENT

World Bank: Agree

MANAGEMENT RESPONSE

Management is developing proposals to implement a Bank-wide procurement information and tracking system, addressing the issues IEG has identified. Decisions on the timing of information system changes will need to be taken in the context of evolving fiscal priorities.

Chairperson's Summary: Committee on Development Effectiveness

The Committee on Development Effectiveness (CODE) met to discuss *The World Bank and Public Procurement: An Independent Evaluation* and the draft Management Response.

Summary

The Committee welcomed the Independent Evaluation Group (IEG) evaluation and endorsed its findings and recommendations. Members agreed that the evaluation served as an important input into the development of the proposed new framework for operational procurement. They welcomed management's assurance that next steps in the reform process would take into account IEG's findings. Members appreciated that the report confirmed the findings of management's extensive stakeholder consultations. The Committee acknowledged that the Bank has been a leader in procurement over time and welcomed management's intention to take on new, innovative approaches to remain at the forefront. They noted the need for the Bank to establish a system that evolves, adjusts, and addresses the challenges, needs, and systemic issues of client countries and moves away from a project/transaction-focused system. Members underscored that reform is not only about rules and procedures, but also about how they are interpreted and applied throughout the procurement life cycle. Particularly, members reinforced the need to build capacity in client countries and among staff; move toward country systems to the extent possible; ensure clear accountability and decision-making structures; and take a fresh approach to risk management.

Members urged a more strategic approach to capacity building to manage procurement and assist clients vis-à-vis strengthening governance and public finance management. They encouraged management to be purposeful in building sustained capacity through country partnerships, lending engagements, and diagnostics. They noted that the Bank would need to undertake country-specific dialogues and ensure it has the appropriate instruments in place to provide clients with the necessary advice and institution-building support.

Members supported moving toward greater use of country systems to the extent possible, under a best-fit-for-purpose approach. They noted that use of country systems is not an either/or issue; rather it is about designing a sensible approach that involves well-calculated risks to achieve greater development impact. Members concurred that the procurement guidelines need to be revised and modernized. They noted management's confirmation that under a fit-for-purpose approach, the revised guidelines will be one of several different procurement arrangements used to support operations under the Bank's Investment Project Finance and will remain in place as a default. They advocated flexibility in the implementation of the guidelines, with clear and adaptable guidance to staff established within the policy.

Members agreed that the Bank should take a more risk-based approach in its procurement procedures to free up resources to focus on higher value-added activities and make the Bank faster and more efficient in project implementation. They subscribed to the need to shift resources toward higher-risk operations and reduce review of lower-value contracts. They encouraged clearer guidance to staff in this respect.

Members noted the importance of ensuring that the principles of value for money and development impact are fully integrated into procurement reform.

Juan José Bravo
CHAIRPERSON

Contents of the Complete Evaluation

Boxes

Figures

Tables

Appendixes

Volume II: Achieving Development Effectiveness through Procurement in Bank Financial Assistance

Figures

Tables

Appendixes

The World Bank Group and Public Procurement

Good public procurement practices are a major determinant of the effectiveness of public expenditure. Effective policies enable better use of government budgets and are therefore an essential element of the poverty reduction focus of the World Bank. More effective public procurement in countries may also allow procurement practices in the World Bank lending to be unified and harmonized with other donors.

Two overarching questions form the core of this evaluation: To what extent has the World Bank helped countries develop better procurement capacity and improve their public procurement systems? And to what extent does the application of World Bank procurement policies in its investment lending help support its own development objectives?

World Bank contributions to the procurement process in countries have taken the form of both advisory services and support through lending. IEG reviews the nature and quality of diagnostic work as well as loans focused on procurement reform — and the impact in terms of results.

IEG's findings lead to a number of recommendations that focus on developing plans and projects in the context of country strategies and implementing changes along prevailing best practices. The recommendations are specific to World Bank systems, although the challenges and issues of effective and transparent procurement are not. Lessons from this evaluation can be applied to improve procurement practices in any system.

ISBN 978-1-4648-0123-5

90000

9 781464 801235

SKU 210123

WORLD BANK GROUP

www.ingramcontent.com/pod-product-compliance
Lightning Source LLC
Chambersburg PA
CBHW080002280326
41935CB00013B/1728